PRACTICAL MARKETING

PRACTICAL MARKETING

a step by step guide to effective planning

DAVID H BANGS

**KOGAN
PAGE**

First published in the United States of America in 1987
by Upstart Publishing Company Inc, Portsmouth, New Hampshire 03801, USA.

Copyright © David H Bangs Jr and Upstart Publishing Co Inc 1987

This edition first published in Great Britain in 1989 by
Kogan Page Limited, 120 Pentonville Road, London N1 9JN.

British Library Cataloguing in Publication Data
Bangs, David H.
    Practical marketing: a step-by-step guide to effective planning.
    1. Marketing. Planning
    I. Title
    658.8'02

    ISBN 0-7494-0036-6

Typeset in Baskerville by BookEns, Saffron Walden, Essex
Printed and bound in Great Britain by Biddles Limited, Guildford

◄ CONTENTS ►

◀ FOREWORD ▶

Entrepreneurial enthusiasm is both an asset and a liability.

All too often, the entrepreneurial enthusiasm which gives birth to a company, and drives it through its earliest successes, contributes to the firm's eventual demise. Often this is due to the entrepreneur's preoccupation with 'product' and 'process'. In the quest for producing a new and better product or service, the entrepreneur tends to overlook whether or not a market actually exists for the product – or whether the product can be brought to market in a profitable way.

Practical Marketing is valuable because it can help businesses to avoid expensive mistakes – and the pain that results from them. This book guides the entrepreneur or manager painlessly through the process of (a) identifying the product, (b) analysing the firm's market and competitive position, and (c) focusing upon the firm's strengths. The book succeeds because it presents sophisticated marketing theory in a non-threatening, interactive way.

Practical Marketing is based on a series of questions which even the most product-oriented entrepreneur will be able to answer. In answering these questions – and learning why they were asked – the entrepreneur will be exposed and sensitised to a new way of looking at products and services, markets, and the competition. After reading the book, the entrepreneur will be less concerned with the specifics of producing a particular widget or service and more concerned with questions such as:

- ☐ Do widget buyers actually exist?
- ☐ Do we have a product which satisfies their needs?
- ☐ Do we have the resources necessary to reach widget buyers?
- ☐ Who else is making widgets?
- ☐ How does our widget differ from theirs?
- ☐ Why should people buy our widgets instead of theirs?

In answering these questions, readers will not only gain a firmer understanding of the tasks which lie ahead in advertising and promoting their product or service, they'll be preparing a comprehensive marketing plan which managers of any *Times 1000* company would be proud to present to their shareholders and senior management.

The most important books are those which cause long-lasting attitude changes. Unfortunately, few marketing books are able to fundamentally change the typical entrepreneur's basic preoccupation with product and process. This is because most marketing texts are so theoretical that entrepreneurs have difficulty relating them to their daily duties. This book succeeds, however, because it is based entirely on defining and meeting particular marketing challenges. This increases the reader's involvement and helps the book to drive home its lessons in the most powerful way possible.

Working through the steps outlined here can contribute to entrepreneurial success – as well as prevent unnecessary hardships and financial loss. *Practical Marketing* should be required reading for new managers and entrepreneurs and recommended reading for seasoned business people who may have forgotten some of the basics necessary for continued business success.

Roger C Parker

◀ INTRODUCTION ▶

'What needs improving at your business? Marketing and sales capability was the response given most by nearly 1,300 executives – 70 per cent of them at small firms – who responded to a poll by the CPA firm of Ernst & Whinney . . .'

The Wall Street Journal, 6 February 1984

A marketing plan is a detailed, written plan that lays out the steps that your company must take to create customers, thereby achieving its sales and marketing objectives.

Good marketing calls for the performance of many small tasks thoroughly and intelligently. Excellent marketing also requires you to have good products or services, and know your customers and prospects better than your competitors do.

Once you analyse your products or services, customers and prospects, and understand what your competitors are up to, you can develop effective strategies to achieve your sales and marketing goals. Most small business owners don't bother to take these extra steps, preferring to press ahead and either copy someone else or take unnecessary chances. This might be called the 'Man of Action' problem, since so many small business owners pride themselves on being doers instead of thinkers.

Actually, you have to be both to succeed in business. First, you need a plan, so that your marketing efforts are not random decisions. Then you have to act to make your plans work.

We worked with a small accountancy firm to create the marketing plan used as the example in this book. Accountancy firms have especially acute marketing problems, since they sell intangible services. What's more, accounting services are almost impossible to differentiate. Accounting reports (tax, financial, management information) all look more or less alike. But the principles of marketing apply in all businesses. What are you selling? Who buys from you? Is the business profitable – or can it become profitable? How do you let people know what you have for sale? Why should they buy from you?

The above-mentioned accountants set their goals and established the action steps needed to reach them. By following their reasoning – and filling in the blank forms provided in Appendix 3 – you can create an effective marketing plan suited to your goals and resources.

This will create a significant marketing edge for you. It doesn't matter what your business is. You can own a shoe shop, a grocery, a restaurant, an employment agency or a dental practice. It doesn't matter. Your competitors probably don't organise their business on marketing principles. In effect, they create customers for you to profit from. All you have to do is follow the steps outlined in this book, develop strategies for your business, and then implement those strategies. This isn't easy – but it winds up being a lot easier than proceeding without a clear marketing plan. And a lot more profitable.

Whatever you do, don't fall into the trap of looking at marketing as a luxury that you can cut at the first sign of a sales slump. Marketing is an investment in your future business. No matter how good your product or service may be, or how outstanding your location, you will still have to practise careful marketing.

Slow sales and slumping profits are marketing problems. Loss of market share is a marketing problem.

If you want to increase your sales, profits and market share, then increase and improve your marketing efforts. Use an expert if you can't do it yourself. But don't do what too many small business owners do: Do not stop marketing efforts because 'you can't afford marketing'. That's a false economy of the worst kind. It will put you out of business.

◀ CHAPTER 1 ▶

MARKETING OVERVIEW

The sole purpose of your business is to create customers.

Technological excellence, delivery capability, service skills, pricing theory and product perfection will, at best, gain you nothing if you can't create customers.

'Marketing' is the complex process of creating customers for your products or services. A marketing plan is a written document which helps you to manage this process – including the action steps needed to make the plan work.

Your marketing plan calls for thoughtful answers to 30 major questions. These questions are highlighted throughout this book. A complete list of these questions is provided in Appendix 1.

Writing the plan is easy. You don't write the plan itself until you've done 95 per cent of the work. The difficult part of market planning is a careful analysis of:

1. Your product or service;
2. Your markets and your position in those markets; and
3. Your business's strengths and weaknesses.

The sole purpose of your business is to create customers.

13

Planning cannot be done in a vacuum. The first step is to take a broad overview of your marketing efforts (including your current markets and your products or services) in the context of current economic and competitive conditions.

Begin by answering the following questions. Don't aim for 100 per cent accuracy. You can fine tune your answers later.

Question 1: What business are you in?

If you have written a business plan, you have already gone through this exercise. If not, ask:

☐ *What are your products/services?* Your business definition is based on what you sell.
☐ *Who are your customers?* Your present customer base and the target markets you want to serve help focus the definition further.
☐ *Why do your customers buy from you?* There are plenty of competitors for every business, and a wide range of other products and services for your customers and prospects to buy.
☐ *What sets your business apart from your competitors?* What's distinct or unusual about your business? If you can differentiate yourself from your competitors in the eyes of your market, you gain a strong advantage.

Your definition of your business will decide the direction your business takes. If you can state clearly and succinctly what you sell, to whom, and why they buy from you, you are well on the way to creating an effective marketing plan.

If you can state clearly and succinctly what you sell, to whom, and why they buy from you, you are well on the way to creating an effective marketing plan.

Imagine yourself travelling in a plane. You strike up a conversation with the person sitting next to you, who asks, 'What business are you in?' How would you answer? Your response should be brief, but clear and specific.

There is no 'right' answer. A series of answers evolves as your business changes. Your products/services and markets change. So does your competitive position. Other people will copy what you do well, and compete for your customers on price, quality, service or wherever you appear vulnerable.

All your market planning efforts are an attempt to elaborate on your answer to that seemingly simple question, 'What business are you in?'

Question 2: What do you sell?
What are you selling? Computers? Landscape designs? Property? Clothing? Legal advice? Fish? Dental services? Golf clubs?

In Chapter 2 you will return to your product/service list from a different angle. For now, just list the products/services you sell in Figure 1.2.

Question 3: What are your target markets?
Target marketing is a simple concept. You have a limited marketing budget. Your business has a potential market consisting of a vaguely defined group of people who might buy your products. In order to invest your money wisely you have to narrow that broad group down to those people (or people in particular institutions) most likely to buy from you.

Many potential buyers are too far away geographically, can't afford your prices, don't want to change suppliers, prefer to deal locally, or are unlikely to become your customers for other reasons. Recognising these limitations on your market is the first step towards target marketing. Next, identify the segments of the overall market which are most likely to buy from you. (See Chapter 3, pages 46–9 for more on this.)

What is target marketing? Look at Figure 1.1. The bull's-eye is worth £10 in sales, the first ring £5, the next ring £3, the outside ring £1. Missing the target is a dead loss.

Now suppose you need £100 in sales to break even, and a marketing budget of £15 (for the sake of the illustration, think of that as 15 arrows). In order to meet your £100 goal, you need five bull's-eyes and 10 arrows in the £5 first ring. Any misses and you can't achieve your goal of £100. Needless to say, you'd take considerable care with each arrow.

To push the simile a bit further, you would find that your marksmanship improves with practice, that taking careful note of surrounding conditions is important, and that focusing on your target pays off. Shooting at one random target after another is harder, and makes your expensively gathered experience useless. So does changing your bow, or forgetting to keep the score.

In marketing, you have to keep track of what you're up to. Fashions change. The economic climate changes. Products and services gain and lose value. Markets shift. But you will always have a finite number of arrows (pounds in your marketing budget), and you will always find that once you have the range on a target it pays to keep shooting at that target until you have good reasons to shoot at a new one.

Figure 1.1 *Target marketing*

Target marketing is a continuous process. You want to know:

1. What are your products and services? You've made a first shot at this one.
2. Who is most likely to buy them from you?
3. What characteristics (wants, needs, habits and so forth) do your customers and hottest prospects share? Segment or differentiate the market.
4. How big are your marketing segments?
5. What is the most profitable segment mix, in terms of ease and cost of sales, sales volume, and price? Rank the segments in terms of potential profitability for your business.

For each product/service, what are the target markets? Jot them down on Figure 1.2.

Figure 1.2 *Product/Service and market list*

If you have many products/services, try to bundle them together into no more than 10 categories. You can always expand the list later – but for now, keep it simple.

Product/Service	Target markets
1. Business consulting	
2. Monthly accounting services	Manufacturers,
3. Audits	service firms,
4. Tax return preparation	and retailers
5. Tax consultation + representation	with sales of
6. Special projects	£ 100,000 to
7. Other accounting services	£ 5,000,000
8.	
9.	
10.	

Question 4: What are your marketing goals for next year? Your sales and profit goals?

You need two sets of goals: for your business and for yourself. Your personal goals come first. You want to be sure you don't commit your business to a strategy which runs counter to your personal wishes. Do you want to sell your business in a few years and retire? Build the business to *Times 1000* size, or keep it small? Be a technological trail-blazer? All of these have been cited by small business owners, and each has profound marketing implications.

Figure 1.3   *Your personal goals*

1. How much money do you want, or need, to earn? *£60,000*

---

2. What sort of lifestyle is desirable for you and your family? *Affluent*

---

3. How big do you want your business to be? *Sales of £250,000*

---

4. How will your business reflect you and your values? *I want to be fair to my employees and my clients*

5. What are your risk parameters? What is your tolerance for risk? *Ours is not a business to take risks—we need achievable goals*

6. What do you want to achieve in five years? *Semi-retirement*

You need two sets of goals for your business. Your personal goals come first.

Some plausible marketing goals for the immediate future are increased revenue or unit sales, improved market share, greater profits, entry into new markets, abandoning a current market, and adopting a new technology or product line. Perhaps you want to improve your company's image, advertising, or promotional efforts. Or implement a new pricing strategy or distribution process.

Be general. These goals will be re-examined and refocused. To turn these vague goals into real objectives, you have to do more. Objectives involve specific numbers and time frames. For now, you will jot down the broad marketing goals you would like to achieve over the next year and over the next three years in Figure 1.5.

Sales and profit goals can be more precise.

If you have a small number of product/service lines, break the goals down further. But even an aggregate number is helpful; you can break it down later. For each product/service and target market of Figure 1.2, forecast sales for the next year in Figure 1.4. A worst-case, best-case, most-likely-case approach makes this somewhat easier and more accurate than just guessing. A product-by-product approach produces a more accurate forecast than lumping all your sales together in one undifferentiated heap.

Figure 1.4 overleaf.

Figure 1.4 *Sales approach*

For each product/service or product line, estimate what sales would be if everything goes wrong next year. Then estimate what sales would be if everything goes perfectly. Since neither case is likely, an in-between sales figure will be a more accurate forecast.

Sales forecast

	Worst case	Most likely case	Best case
Product/Service			
1. Business consulting	£25,000	£30,000	£40,000
2. Monthly accounting services	£25,000	£30,000	£40,000
3. Audits	£10,000	£20,000	£30,000
4. Tax return preparation	£25,000	£30,000	£30,000
5. Tax consultation + representation	£20,000	£25,000	£30,000
6. Special projects	£15,000	£20,000	£30,000
7. Other accounting services	£15,000	£20,000	£25,000
TOTAL:	£135,000	£175,000	£225,000

Profit goals are harder to establish. If you know what profit you traditionally make as a percentage of sales, use the sales forecast and add a bit. You don't want to set goals too low, and you will (you hope) become more profitable with more sales. Experience and time will correct or corroborate your hopes.

Note that Figure 1.5 gives you both a revenue figure and a time frame. This makes your broad objectives more precise, which helps you to set up benchmarks to test progress and measure improvement.

Figure 1.5 *Preliminary marketing, sales and profit goals*

Marketing goals

1. Develop a programme for small business financial management

2. _____

3. Develop a programme for more management consulting and less accounting

Sales goals for each product/service (see Figure 1.4 for next year's most likely figures)

1. Business consulting   £ 30,000   £ 45,000

2. Monthly accounting services   £ 30,000   £ 45,000

3. Audits   £ 20,000   £ 40,000

4. Tax return preparation   £ 30,000   £ 35,000

5. Tax consultation & representation   £ 25,000   £ 35,000

6. Special projects   £ 20,000   £ 35,000

7. Other accounting services   £ 20,000   £ 30,000

Profit goals   £ 175,000   £ 265,000
£ 50,000 profit   at least £100,000

Comments:_____
_____
_____
_____
_____

Question 5: What might keep you from achieving these goals?

Possible barriers include cash flow problems or capital shortages, personnel deficiencies or inefficiencies, weak technology, stale product lines, pricing woes, declining or flat sales, strong new competitors, quality control problems, and many more.

A wise small business owner or manager knows what the problems are and addresses them.

Every company has limitations. A wise small business owner or manager knows what the problems are and addresses them. The ostrich-like manager, on the other hand, is always receiving nasty surprises.

Some problems are long term. A jobbing printer has to be concerned about laser printing, not because the technology is widespread but because it will be, and it will change his or her business. Being a supplier to a declining industry is a long-term problem. So is being located in a stagnant or declining local economy.

Product and service limitations might involve quality control, rejected raw materials stock, stock-outs, delivery problems, lack of skilled service personnel, or old equipment that puts you at a time and cost disadvantage.

Know your limitations. Then correct them – or adjust your marketing plans to accommodate them. Follow Figure 1.6 and keep a list of problems that you think might get between you and your goals. The finest memory is not so firm as faded ink. Write them down.

Figure 1.6 *Obstacles we could face*

Today's date: 5 / 2 / 89

What problems am I avoiding?

1. *Cash flow*: slow paying clients; collections are difficult
2. *Educational updates*: necessary but difficult to produce
3. *Setting clear, consistent fees*

What problems might prevent us from reaching our marketing, sales, and profit goals?

1. _Time_ ⎱ _we have a vicious circle!_
2. _Being understaffed_ ⎰ _Once our cash flow is up,_
3. _____ _then we can deal with_
4. _____ _these problems_
5. _____

What are we going to do about these problems?

1. Assign responsibility to individuals to achieve solutions.
2. Allocate resources and authority to these people.
3. Establish benchmarks and deadlines to help them monitor their progress.

We want to increase our cash flow in 3 months, and we want to add more personnel in 6 months.

Note that Figure 1.6 calls for action. A marketing plan has to be implemented, or it's a waste of time. Dramatic changes in your business will come from correcting errors and problems. More lasting and profitable, if less spectacular, changes result from implementing a carefully thought-out marketing strategy.

> Marketing is as much a cost of doing business as rent or payroll.

Question 6: What is your marketing budget?
This is a trick question. If you have a marketing budget, you can answer it. If you don't, you have the most common problem: no budget at all. The second most common small business budgeting problem is relying on a reactive, sloppy, 'whatever is available if I have no better use for it' excuse for a budget.

Marketing is as much a cost of doing business as rent or payroll. It isn't a cost centre to cut at the first sign of a sales slump or reduce to boost profits for a month or two. If you don't have a

23

marketing budget, or if you think your current budget needs improvement, go no further. You have to have a budget – unless you want to waste money and forgo sales and profit improvement.

Anyone can set a budget. Setting a budget worth following requires a lot of skill.

One more common method of setting a marketing budget is to allocate a fixed percentage of forecast sales on a calendar basis. You can get trade figures. Ask your business adviser, accountant, bank manager or other financial experts such as editors of trade magazines. Ask other successful business owners. These figures will provide some useful guidelines.

Just remember that more than advertising and public relations come out of your marketing budget. What do sales cost you? Sales training? Preparation of window displays? Sales support and presentation pieces? Check through Figure 1.7. Your marketing budget has to reflect your business, not someone else's.

Look at your marketing, sales, and profit goals in Figure 1.5. Try to work out what it will cost to reach them. If it is more than you can afford, fine. That forces some choices upon you. You need a marketing budget you can live with, one that helps you to reach your goals and doesn't tie you to a formula that can't adjust to sudden shifts.

The best marketing budgets have two parts: first, a fixed monthly amount to meet ongoing, monthly marketing expenses; second, a contingency or project budget to help you to meet unexpected marketing needs. A new market may open up, a competitor may retire, or new competition may appear. How you respond to these opportunities and challenges is heavily influenced by your budget.

You know your marketing, sales, and profit goals. Discuss these with your accountant or business advisers. Marketing without money is like making bricks without straw. It can't be done without divine intervention – and that kind of marketing help cannot be relied on.

Figure 1.7 *Marketing budget items*

This is not an exhaustive list. Use it as a starting point. Your company will use some of these categories plus others peculiar to your marketing needs.

1. Selling (direct costs)
   Sales salaries and commissions £_____
   Travel £ 1,000
   Entertainment £ 2,000
2. Selling (indirect costs)
   Training £_____
   Marketing research £_____
   Statistical analysis £_____
   Subscriptions and dues £ 5,000
3. Advertising £ 2,000
4. Sales promotion other than advertising £10,000
5. Public relations £ 500
6. Shipping and handling
   Order filling, packaging £_____
   Postage and cartage £ 1,800
7. Credits and collection
   Administrative expense £_____
   Bad debt allowance £_____
8. Marketing administration £_____

Incomplete campaigns eat profits, so make sure you have enough money to finish your marketing campaigns.

To set up your budgets, use your resources. Your accountant or financial advisers can help you put actual costs to your goals more efficiently than you can. However, you can provide estimates, based on your goals and prior experience in your business. Sketch in your first rough estimates in Figure 1.8.

Figure 1.8 *Preliminary marketing budget estimates*

Made by: **GL**   Date: **5/2/89**
Reviewed by:_____   Date:_____

Goal or action: (eg, Advertising	Timing: monthly	Costs: £750/month)
Yellow Pages ad	annually	£100/month
Chamber of Commerce	2 ads/year	£50/ad
Brochure		£2,000/year
Brochure mailing	4 times/year	£800/year
Misc ads	2 times/year	£400/year

Total: £ **4,500/year**

Use this for rough estimates only. You need your accountant's help in setting up your final marketing budget.

Summary of Chapter 1

1. Preliminary goals (personal, marketing, sales, profit) have been established for the next year and the next three years (see Figures 1.3 and 1.5).
2. Some problems have been identified and initial corrective steps taken (see Figure 1.6).
3. Your products and services have been listed in Figure 1.2.
4. Your target markets have been identified and linked with your products/services in Figure 1.2.
5. A marketing budget estimate has been made in Figure 1.8.

In Appendix 3, fill in copies of Figures 1.2, 1.3, 1.5, 1.6 and 1.8 to refer to in subsequent chapters. Your marketing plan will grow from these initial assumptions and estimates.

A list of effective small business marketing strategies is given in Chapter 8 (see Figure 8.4 on page 127). As you work through the planning process, your strategic choices will begin to emerge.

◀ CHAPTER 2 ▶

PRODUCTS AND SERVICES

If you are already in business, you already have products/services, markets and problems. If you are about to begin a business, you probably have a clear idea of what, where, when, and to whom you will be selling.

The leading theoretical approach to marketing demands that you first establish what your markets want, then provide a way to satisfy them profitably. That's fine if you have the luxury of choosing your target market and product/service mix. Most of us, though, are limited by our experience and interests, to say nothing of other limitations such as money, family obligations and so forth.

What can you do if you are already in business? Make haste slowly. Change gradually to a marketing orientation. Understand your target markets in depth, and measure the products/services you offer against the demands of those markets. You can change product and service lines over time to meet the changing demands of your customers and prospects. But you can't suddenly switch – it takes planning and time.

There are powerful constraints on the kinds of product and service you can offer: money, time, customer habits, competition, and technology are a few. Creating demand for a new product

> People buy solutions to their problems and satisfaction for their wants and needs.

27

and changing consumer buying habits is close to impossible. Introducing a new technology can bankrupt you. The number of truly innovative products or services introduced each year is tiny, and beyond the scope of this book.

Most products and services offered by small businesses are generic. While you may think that your products and services are special, that perception is not necessarily shared by your market.

To gain a competitive advantage you must do two things:

1. Know your products/services better than the competition know theirs.
2. Know the benefits of your products/services from your customers' perspective.

Understand the benefits your customers can get from your products or services. Look at your business from their point of view. Without a strong reason to think otherwise, one hardware shop is like another, solicitors are interchangeable; fishmongers are where you buy fish. What's so special about your screwdrivers, or your wills, or your halibut?

People buy benefits. What they want is not necessarily what you think you are selling. They buy solutions to their problems. They buy satisfaction of needs and wants. The solutions and satisfactions are the benefits they buy along with your products/services.

The more reasons to buy you can communicate to your target markets the better.

Question 7: What are the benefits provided by your products/services?
A careful product/service line analysis goes beyond a list of what you currently sell, and far beyond product knowledge. Not that these are unimportant pieces of information – in fact, that's where product/service line analysis begins.

1. *List the products/services you currently sell.* (Go back and refer to

28

Figure 1.2.) You may want to reorganise or recategorise them, or add to your list. Enter the products or services on Figure 2.4.

Before you can match up products/services and markets, you have to form a clear idea of what needs and wants those products and services satisfy. Any product or service can satisfy a number of wants and needs. While people don't always know why they buy what they buy, you can draw some useful conclusions by observing and enquiring.

Think of several applications for each product or service, and several sets of wants and needs they satisfy. By communicating this to your target markets, you greatly increase the market appeal of those products and services. The more reasons to buy you can communicate to your target markets the better.

2. *For each product or service, ask: What is its purpose?* What needs or wants does it satisfy for your customers? For your prospects? Jot down the most obvious needs and wants that each product or service satisfies on Figure 2.4. This will give you a better understanding of the markets you can reasonably target and provide the underpinnings of your marketing strategy.

What kinds of wants and needs should you consider in Figure 2.4? Marketing gurus have listed thousands. A handful are offered in Figure 2.1.

3. *For each product or service, ask: Is it a breadwinner now, or will it be in the future? Is it past its prime? Should it be continued? Or given more support (financial, personnel, promotion)?* You want to put your resources to work where they'll have the best long-term pay-off.

4. *Should you expand your current product/service lines?* Sometimes sales of one product reveal customer needs for another. If a significant number of your customers ask for a product that would be an extension of your current lines, the risk of extending your product lines may be worth taking. It takes less effort to cross-sell your old customers than it does to create new ones.

Ask product line questions quarterly. We get so attached to the old product line that we forget to update it. Meanwhile the market moves away.

5. *What are the particular advantages/disadvantages of each product or service compared with competitive products and services?* Product/service comparisons tip you off to competitive positioning. In Chapter 4, Competitive Analysis, further marketing comparisons will help to keep you ahead of the competition. For now, take special note of differences in target markets and benefits advertised.

Figure 2.1. *Why do people buy things?*

Even though individuals ultimately make all purchasing decisions, their approach will differ depending on whether they are buying for themselves or buying for their company or institution. Several ways of looking at buyer wants and needs are shown here.

Basis for wanting things:
1. To fulfil biological needs
2. To gain security
3. To get status
4. To gain recognition
5. To satisfy aggression
6. To satisfy sensibilities
7. To lessen anxiety
8. To save time

Some buyer motivations:
1. Satisfaction of the senses
2. Imitation of other people
3. Stylishness
4. Profit
5. Convenience
6. Knowledge
7. Comfort
8. Fear
9. Pride
10. Curiosity

11. Pleasure
12. Self-expression or self-fulfilment
13. Gaining an advantage
14. Saving money

For institutional markets, important motivations to buy include:
1. Dependability
2. Discounts for bulk orders
3. Price and quality
4. Relationship with current vendors
5. Customisation
6. Market exclusivity
7. Value
8. Delivery schedules
9. Guarantees
10. Safety for the purchasing agent ('You don't get in trouble buying IBM . . .' attitude is a good example of bureaucratic thinking. The IBM choice isn't necessarily the best, but it's viewed as defensible.)

Figure 2.2 *Product comparison form*

Fill this in for each product or service you offer. For the sake of simplicity, compare yours only with the leading competitive products or services.

Product/Service: ___All our accounting services___

	Yours	The competition's
Target markets:	Mfg, service and retail co's w/sales of £700,000 to £5,000,000	Large corporations & their executives; some small businesses
Benefits offered:		
1.	Aggressive sales approach	Passive sales approach
2.	Timely service	→
3.	Use of computers	→
Quality	Very good	→
Price	On low side	Higher fees

31

	Yours	The competition's
Improved versions		
Location	Convenient – will visit client when necessary →	
Delivery	Meet clients dead lines →	
Follow-up service	Excellent	Good
Availability	Very good	Good
Convenience		
Reliability	Good ————→	
Service	Excellent	Depends how big account is
Guarantees	No satisfaction, no charge	?
Other (specify)		
1.	Experience with small business owners	Not as much experience with this market
2.	Creative approach to solving clients' problems	Defensive approach
3.		

Target market and benefit differences are important pieces of information for your marketing plans.

Making comparisons, you may discover new applications, new product ideas, new opportunities. Look outside your business. Maybe the competition has a wider line, or a more specialised line. Would this make sense for your business? Perhaps their packaging is better, or their distribution or delivery system superior. Perhaps their advertising is stronger. Adapt Figure 2.2 to compare product mix, product lines, or other areas where you might be able to gain a competitive edge.

6. *Have you made improvements to your products or services lately? Are you planning any?* You don't want your products and services to become stale, or outmoded, or be made obsolete by your competitors' changes. This is more than a question of style or fads. 'New! Improved!' is a great marketing line, especially if the product or service is really new and improved. Improvements

are a powerful positioning tool. Who doesn't want the improved model?

7. *What new products and services are you planning?* Should you develop new ones? Fill out a product line? Meet competition? Or should you prune back your product line to the most profitable elements?

One of the most powerful marketing strategies for small businesses is to locate and dominate market niches too small or too specialised for bigger companies to invade profitably. Quite often this calls for new products or highly specialised skill sets. However, any new product or service cries out for strong marketing justification. Otherwise, it's all too easy to squander your resources on exciting but unprofitable new ventures.

8. *What are possible substitutes for your goods or services?* Are there any new developments (technological, social, economic) that might result in new ways of satisfying your market's wants and needs?

Not all dangers and opportunities are obvious. The only way to keep abreast of what might affect your business is to read, attend trade or other business exhibitions, and keep your eyes and ears open. Your chances of picking up an opportunity are far greater than your competitors' if you periodically review and analyse your product and service lines.

9. *Can you list at least five new applications for your products/services?* Repackaged products or new applications of old products open up new marketing opportunities. For the product grid (Figure 2.7), think of new applications as new products.

Huge marketing gains have come from new applications of old products and services. You can sometimes repackage or reposition a product or service to appeal to a wider market, or to deepen penetration of your current markets. A classic example of repackaging is baking powder, which now sells more widely in the US as a refrigerator cleaner and air freshener than it ever did as a baking aid.

Ask questions. Ask your customers, suppliers, sales force and other interested parties what your products and services might be used for. Their answers might provide new applications that result in tomorrow's sales.

Your aim is to develop an image of offering something special.

Use the answers and ideas you generate to fill in Figure 2.3 for each product or service.

Figure 2.3 *Product/Service application worksheet*

Product/Service: _Accounting and management advisory services_

What are its features? _Preparing tax returns and financial statements; analyse cash flow; balance sheet; make recommendations_

What benefits does it produce? _Helps business owner save money and use his/her financial resources better_

How is it used? _When client needs help solving problems_

How is it purchased (unit, bulk, with other products)? Which other products? _With other services, usually as a result of doing their tax returns_

What are other possible applications of this product/service? _Could apply to personal financial planning for business owners — we could offer appropriate services._

Use these ideas to rethink how your products might be marketed. As an example, in the USA, basketballs are used as float valves in some industrial applications. Their features of toughness, uniform size and quality, roundness and buoyancy make them ideal for this purpose.

Now put the two concepts together: What wants and needs do your products fill? Who might have these wants and needs?

Question 8: What is special about your products/services?
What is the 'unique selling proposition' for your product and service lines? For each product and service? Is it quality? Price? Convenience? Style? Professionalism? What sets your products and services apart from the rest? The information gathered in Figure 2.2 helps you determine the unique selling proposition of your products.

Your aim is to develop an image of offering something special. Your local mini supermarket has a unique selling proposition: You can get a loaf of bread or a jar of marmalade without getting your car out, and at odd hours. Look at competing businesses and ask what's special about them. Can those insights help you to position and define your business? Every business has something special to recommend it. What's your claim?

You may want to stress quality, or dominate your market through price competition.

Figure 2.4 overleaf.

Figure 2.4 *Product/Service benefits and markets*

Your product/service	Benefits it offers (wants/needs fulfilled)	Possible target markets
1. Business consulting	solves business owners' problems	Retail,
2. Monthly accounting services	keeps books up to date	manufacturing
3. Audits	keeps clients from worrying; saves them £	and service firms
4. Tax return preparation	Tax return is done correctly	with sales
5. Tax consultation and representation	keeps clients from worrying; saves them £	of
6. special projects	fulfils that clients specific need	£700,000 to
7. Other accounting services	client can have whatever is needed	£5,000,000
8.		
9.		
10.		

Some ways to set your products apart from the competition:

1. *New, improved.* Oven cleaners were messy, dangerous and splattery. They are now sprayed on straight from the can. Lotus in the US took spreadsheets for microcomputers a step further than the competition, and dominated the market for business software.

2. *Packaging.* Higher profits will often come simply from better packaged goods, sold at a higher price, rather than a better product.

3. *Pricing.* BIC grabbed the cheap pen market with their low-priced ballpoint. On the other hand, lack of courage in pricing is a major weakness for small business. Expensive cars may cost only £500 more to manufacture than cheap models; the price differential can be thousands of pounds. Price and image march together.

4. *Advertising* and *promotion.* What really is the difference between one fast food chain and another? It will not be the beef or the chickens they sell but will be the *perceived* value – as advertised and promoted.

5. *Delivery.* Retail stores all over the world are being hurt by direct marketing. It's the fastest growing retail segment. Hundreds of merchants let you shop at home, and will quickly deliver their products to your door – see the ads in every colour supplement or in your credit card envelope.

6. *Convenience.* Look at direct marketing again. Or check out your local late-opening shop. Many banks are now open for more convenient hours due to the press of competition. A bank that opens Saturday morning has a big advantage over a bank that doesn't.

7. *Follow-up service.* After-sale efforts are strong product/service differentiators. Most people will buy a brand of washing machine if they can rely on after-sale service. This contrasts sharply with discount stores. Both after-sale service and price chopping are valid marketing strategies. But it is possible to make more money in the long run by stressing service, not price. A dental practice that routinely involves its patients in their own health care by sending reminders will lose fewer patients than one that saves money by not keeping in touch.

Question 9: Which product/service is the best contributor to your overheads and profits? Which product/service is the biggest drain on your overheads and profits?

This is a simple accounting question. If you cannot tell quickly which product/service you sell makes the most money (net of all expenses, including marketing and sales costs, bad debts and so forth), then you had better have a talk with your accountant. This is important information with direct marketing implications. Where do you make money? Where do you lose money? How can you do more of the former and less of the latter – ie, can you ride your strong products more? Cull the losers? Who buys the good products? Who buys the 'bad' ones?

Figure 2.5 *Winners and losers*

Products/services with major impact on overheads and profits:

	Contributors	Amounts
1.	Business consulting	£ 30,000
2.	Monthly accounting services	30,000
3.	Audits	20,000
4.	Tax consultation + representation	25,000
5.	Special projects	20,000

	Detractors	Amounts
1.	Individual's tax returns	£ 9,000
2.		
3.		
4.		
5.		

Know what your products and services contribute to or take away from your business.

Label your products and services as cash cows, dogs, rising stars, and owner's ego. Cash cows are products that give you a good profit for very little effort. Dogs are money losers. Rising stars are tomorrow's cash cows. And owner's ego products or services are tomorrow's dogs, unless they fit in with wider company objectives.

For now, keep it simple. What products and services make money for you? What products or services don't?

There may be excellent reasons to lose money for a while: gaining market share, acquiring mastery of a new technology or learning new skills, building today for tomorrow's profit. So a current loser is not necessarily either a dog or owner's ego. Nor is a current winner necessarily good. You may be missing out on tomorrow's markets by keeping a product too long.

The important point is to know what your products and services contribute or take away from your business.

Figure 2.6 *Product/Service matrix*

The last piece of the product/service puzzle is to look at the Product/Service grid, Figure 2.7. Where do your leading products and services fall on this grid? Your aim is to increase sales and profits. There are four basic ways to do this.

Figure 2.7 *Product/Service grid*

	Core markets	New target markets
P	Old product/service	Old product/service
R	old customers	new customers
O	(lowest risk)	(risky)
D		
U	New product/service	New product/service
C	old customers	new customers
T	(risky)	(riskiest)

Selling new products to new customers is as risky as starting a new business.

Ask yourself how you could sell old products to new customers, or new products to old customers, before even considering selling new products to new customers. Increasing sales of old products to old customers is normally the safest way to increase sales, but may not provide a sufficiently large gain. Selling new products to new customers is as risky as starting a new business – perhaps riskier, because it can sap your energy at the expense of your current business.

All of this leads to Figure 2.8, New product/service objectives. If you decide to make product or service changes, or want to provide new goodies for your target markets to purchase, treat these changes as seriously as any other major change in your business. Set objectives, including costs, deadlines and responsibility. Implement changes carefully and systematically. Don't leave them to chance.

Use all the information gathered so far to flesh out the form. Consider improved or changed products and services to be new products or services.

Figure 2.8 *New product/service objectives*

Person responsible:__RCM_____ Review date:__8/2/89__

Product/service idea:__Business management consulting__

Benefits it will offer:__increased profits, financial strategy improvement, depth of our experience__

Target markets:__garages, dealers__

Timing:__12 months__

Anticipated sales: (£ or unit; by quarter)__£5,000/year minimum__

Anticipated costs: __see__

1. Development __£5,000 to £8,000__

2. Advertising __Direct mail, telemarketing £2,000 to £3,000__

3. Impact on other products/services__Will augment client base__

4. Other (specify)_____

Comments:_____

_____

Action taken:_____

_____

By:_____ Date:_____

Don't hurry with any product change. Mull over the idea for a while. Discuss it. Play the devil's advocate. New products have hidden costs that are difficult to foresee, and seldom pay off as well or as fast as you hope.

Summary of Chapter 2

1. You looked at your products and services and noted the benefits they offer and the target markets which seek those benefits. Keep a copy of Figure 2.4 for reference. Update it as needed.

2. You compared your products and services with those offered by your leading competitors to identify differences and gain preliminary ideas on how to differentiate your business from theirs. Figure 2.2 will help you to identify the unique selling proposition of each product or service, which will be used in setting advertising directions.

3. You looked at each major product and service to find new applications (and new target markets). Figure 2.3 is a piece of the competitive analysis puzzle, as well as a source of new product line or product mix ideas.

4. Risk analysis entered the picture in Figures 2.6 and 2.7.

5. You found competitive strengths and weaknesses in what you market. You will use this in Chapter 6 to help define your competitive position.

6. You outlined new product and service objectives in Figure 2.8. You may have to work these into your sales and profit goals. New products cast long shadows.

Figure 2.9 *A summary of your product/service goals*

Sales goals (for each quarter of
next year, in pounds or in units)

Product/Service:	I	II	III	IV	TOTAL
1. Business consulting	10,000	10,000	10,000	10,000	40,000
2. Monthly Accounting services	10,000	10,000	10,000	10,000	40,000
3. Audits	7,500	7,500	7,500	7,500	30,000
4. Tax return preparation	20,000	2,500	5,000	2,500	30,000
5. Tax consultation and representation	7,500	7,500	7,500	7,500	30,000
6. Special Projects	7,500	7,500	7,500	7,500	30,000
7. Other Accounting services	6,250	6,250	6,250	6,250	25,000

◀ CHAPTER 3 ▶

CUSTOMERS AND PROSPECTS

Your hunches have to be substantiated.

Who wants your goods and services?

You can't know too much about your customers and prospects. This calls for marketing research. Facts and figures elevate your marketing plans from wishful thinking to purposeful action. There is no substitute for hard information.

Your hunches, based on experience and observation, are important. They simplify market research by defining limits and setting directions for further investigation.

But they have to be substantiated. Hunches have an irksome way of being half-truths, and half-truths can be disastrous. 'I feel that there's a big market for this . . .' and 'I have a hunch that we can double sales by . . .' are two of the most common pitfalls for small business owners. Put another way, small businesses aren't destroyed from outside, by competitors or fate. Often, they self destruct.

Figure 3.1 *Marketing research samples*

Marketing research provides answers to questions such as:

1. Who are your best customers and prospects?
2. How does the 80/20 rule (that 80 per cent of your profits come from 20 per cent of your customers) affect you?
3. How do your customers perceive your products/services?
4. What do they want from a business like yours?
5. How can you profitably satisfy their needs and wants?
6. What's the potential of this market?
7. Should you market goods, services, or both?
8. What do your customers read, watch, listen to?

You have to know how your target markets perceive the value of your products/services to make good marketing decisions. If you don't know how your company and its products/services are perceived, you will waste time and aim the wrong products at the wrong markets at the wrong time.

Professional marketing consultants can get this information faster and more cheaply than you can. If your budget is tight, check with local business schools. Marketing academics sometimes do consulting work. Since most basic market research questions are the same, this saves you from reinventing the wheel. It should cost you no more than out-of-pocket expenses. Marketing consultants know the questions to ask and how to get the answers. They will put this information to work, ferreting out better opportunities for you to pursue. This is an added bonus for your marketing research investment.

Your aim is to categorise your current customers as prime, good and others.

Figure 3.2 *Basic marketing research questions*

These are a few questions that basic marketing research will help you to answer.

Information about the buyer:
Age?
Annual income?
Gender?
Ethnic group?
Profession or occupation?
Owner of a home?
Media preferred?

Information about the competition:
Market share?
Advertising plan?
Price strategies?
Distribution?
Length of time in business?

Information about the product:
Benefits?
Price?
Service?
Design specifics?
Where sold?
Packaging?
How will it be used?
How many bought in a year?
What to improve?

Question 10: Who are your current customers?

You can't specify target markets, segment the markets, or otherwise improve your marketing abilities without detailed knowledge of your current customers.

Suppose your market is limited to punk-rock fans. What will you do when the next fad hits? Grow up with your market and change with them? Or cater to the tastes of adolescents forever?

If you sell to industrial companies, who are they? What are their sales levels and geographical distribution? Who makes the buying decision? What market segment buys which products – and what information can these people give you?

If you sell to individual consumers, what are they like? What are the demographics of the market? What are the people's age, gender, income, stage in the life cycle, education level?

Market segmentation is a method of organising and categorising those persons or organisations which you think will buy your products. Look at your customers and note their salient characteristics, then look to wider markets for more groups of people with the same (or similar) characteristics. The usual route is to begin with a fuzzy concept, seek out more detailed information to help define some rough market segments, then refine these into better-defined target markets. This can be entertaining as well as highly rewarding.

The ingenuity of market research professionals is noteworthy. As an example, a research technique called VALS (for Value and Life-Style Study) was developed in America and helped Manufacturers Hanover Trust Company in New York to identify six psychographic groups within one demographic segment – the 'baby boomers'. (Psychographics, a valuable market analysis tool, examines the life-styles and values of various market segments to discover how consumers think and what motivates them.) The upshot was a successful marketing campaign that used only one slogan, 'We realise your potential', to appeal to the six different mindsets. You might be able to benefit from describing your customers and hot prospects using the segmentation criteria in Figure 3.3.

Put these to work for you. Figure 3.4, Market segmentation worksheet, may be helpful. You will probably find that you sell most profitably to certain segments and very poorly to others, which should influence your planning. Think of the 80/20 rule:

80 per cent of your profits come from 20 per cent of your customers. If you can get a good handle on who that profitable 20 per cent is and who the unprofitable 80 per cent is, you will prosper.

Figure 3.3 *Some market segmentation criteria*

Use these categories as criteria to describe your customer base. Look for clusters of people described by these criteria to help direct further marketing efforts.

Demographic
   Age
   Gender
   Income level
   Occupation
   Religion
   Race/ethnic group
   Education
   Social class

Geographic
   Country
   Region
   County
   City/town
   Size of population
   Climate
   Population density

Psychographic
   Leader or follower
   Extrovert or introvert
   Achievement-oriented or content with the status quo
   Independent or dependent
   Conservative or left wing
   Traditional or experimental
   Socially conscious or self-centred

Consumer/Behavioural
   Usage rate
   Benefits sought
   Method of usage
   Frequency of usage
   Frequency of purchase

Business markets
   Type of business (manufacturer, retail, wholesale, service)
   Standard Industrial Classification (SIC) code
   Size of business
   Financial strength
   Number of employees
   Location
   Structure
   Sales level
   Special requirements
   Distribution patterns

Figure 3.4 *Market segmentation worksheet*

Fill in one of these forms for each of your products/services.

By: _GL_____ Date: _10 / 2 /89_____

Product/Service: _All accounting services we offer_

Describe 'ideal customer' according to the criteria listed in Figures 3.2 and 3.3. Entrepreneurs in their late 30s to early 50s; owners of retail, service or manufacturing firms with sales of £700,000 to £5,000,000

Describe their purchasing patterns. When they are aware of their need. They want aggressive and innovative solutions to their problems – they don't have time to research solutions themselves. Often, they need special work performed

What makes them 'ideal customers' for this product/service? They have good ideas and want them implemented. Also they can pay our £5,000 annual fee.

Who buys what, when, where and why are key pieces of marketing information.

49

Question 11: What are their buying habits?

Who buys what, when, where and why are key pieces of marketing information. If you establish nothing more than the answers to these questions, you will be miles ahead of most of your competitors.

Gather the following basic information on each product, product line, or service you offer:

- ☐ Who makes the buying decision?
- ☐ What's the size of the sale in pounds?
- ☐ How many units are sold?
- ☐ What is your cost per sale?
- ☐ What do your customers buy?
- ☐ When do they buy it?
- ☐ Is their purchase seasonal?
- ☐ Why do they buy it?
- ☐ Where do they make the buying decision?
- ☐ How do they finance their purchase?

How do your customers view your products and services? This is a research and development question. If you can define your products from your customers' point of view, you can discover new ways to market your products/services, new target markets, new profitability. For instance, if a customer asks for a refinement of a standard product in your line, can you redesign and repackage that product for other people?

The key marketing point: People buy solutions to problems.

Reworking your basic products and services to fit customer demands can be a powerful marketing tool. Here are some examples:

1. Special containers for cleaning materials and medicines to render them 'childproof'.
2. The continual simplification of microcomputers. The current generation of 'user-friendly' computers is geared to people unfamiliar with computers.

3. Overnight package delivery. One company spotted a market for overnight small package and letter delivery. It was always there; they were just the first to spot it. Their competitors are still catching up.
4. 'Meals on wheels' to busy money market offices (especially in down times).

The key marketing point: people buy solutions to problems. They buy satisfaction of their wants and needs. They don't buy products and services. If your customers have complaints, find out why. What's their problem? How can your company help them to solve that problem?

Question 12: Why do your customers buy your goods/services?
Answer this one correctly and become rich and famous.

How can you find out why people buy from you? Ask them. (Figure 3.5 is a survey that an accountancy practice used for its clients. A generic version of Figure 3.5 appears in Appendix 3.) It helps if you give your customers a structure. This is an area where a professionally developed survey pays off.

When you do a survey make sure to get answers to these three basic questions:

1. Where did you hear of our shop/product/service?
2. What would you like us to offer?
3. How can we serve you better?

In Figure 2.4, you matched products with the needs and wants they fulfil. Now put those insights to work. Who has these needs and wants? Which of your target markets can you satisfy profitably? Perhaps you can reposition some of your products to appeal to these markets. Perhaps you will have to change the product/service mix.

The important thing to keep in mind is that people won't buy goods and services they don't want, no matter how good the advertising and positioning. You can only sell them what they want to buy. Sometimes that will be what they need. But it will very seldom be what you think you are selling.

Some examples: you think you sell a medical service. Your customers think they are buying a solution to a problem, a friendly ear, an antidote to fear. Helena Rubenstein was widely quoted as saying she didn't sell perfume, she sold hope. Coventry sells transport, not cars. Hollywood sells entertainment, not films.

More examples: if you sell to bureaucrats, remember that their number one concern is to be safe. If you sell to teenagers, remember they need to be in step with their peers. If you sell to a local retail customer base, remember that they buy convenience, safety, cleanliness and courtesy along with your groceries or hardware.

Apply this way of thinking to your business. What emotional needs or wants do your products satisfy? What other benefits do they provide? Then match those benefits to your target markets.

How can you discover your market's needs and wants? Ask them. Observe them. Read – trade magazines are full of articles about why people buy, and what triggers their purchasing decisions. Attend trade seminars. Talk to other business owners and managers. Above all, ask your customers.

Figure 3.5 *Client survey*

To our valued clients:

Please take a few minutes to complete this short questionnaire. Our aim is to give you the service you need, want and deserve. Your honest answers to these questions can help us serve you better.

1. How would you rate the quality of work we have performed for you in the past?

   Excellent_____   Good_____   Fair_____   Poor_____

   1A. If not excellent, please explain.

   _____

   _____

2. How would you rate the timeliness of the work we perform for you?

   Excellent_____   Good_____   Fair_____   Poor_____

   2A. If not excellent, please explain.

   _____

   _____

3. What service would you like us to perform for you that we do not offer?

   _____

   _____

4. Please feel free to give us any constructive criticism you feel we could use.

   _____

   _____

5. We plan to begin a seminar series in the not too distant future. What areas would you like to see covered in these seminars?

   _____

   _____

   5A. How interested would you be in attending our seminars?

   Very____   Somewhat____   Little____   Not at all____

Remember why you're in business: to create customers and satisfy them, at an acceptable profit.

Question 13: Who are your best customers and prospects?

Use a straightforward approach. Match the information about the most profitable products with the market segments that purchase those products. If you can find out why they made these purchases and can find other groups, in sufficient numbers, with similar characteristics, then these new groups become your best prospects. With luck, they will turn into your best customers.

This is an endless process. Your target markets change over time; your product lines and mix change; your business changes.

But the basic process remains constant:

1. Identify your profitable products/services, including the 'rising stars'.
2. Find out as much as you can about the people who buy those products/services. Who are they? What are their buying patterns? How often do they buy? How much do they spend? What offers do they respond to?
3. Find other people like them. These are your hot prospects.
4. Identify unprofitable products/services, including the 'dogs' and 'owner's ego'.
5. Find out who buys these products/services – and stop marketing to them, or switch them to more profitable products. This may mean leaving a comfortable market for a profitable one. Remember why you're in business: to create customers and satisfy them, at an acceptable profit.

Question 14: What is your market share?

Market share is the percentage share of total sales to a given market. For example, if you sell £225,000 worth of services annually to a market which buys £1,000,000 worth of that particular service a year, you'd have a 22.5 per cent market share. Market share can be measured in unit sales: 225,000 units out of a total market of 1,000,000 units. Or in purchasing units: 225,000 people out of the total market of 1,000,000 buy your product.

Note that market share presupposes knowledge of the total size of the market, which depends in turn on how you define your target market.

Market share information helps you to decide whether to enter, abandon, invade or protect a market niche. As a rule of thumb, a 25 per cent market share is dominant and makes you a major player in that market. If you can identify a market niche large enough for profitability, yet small enough to be unattractive to big businesses and grab 25 per cent of that market, you have a winner. On the other hand, if your arch rival has 50 per cent of that market, there might not be room for both of you.

Question 14A: Is your market share growing, shrinking, or stable?

Question 14B: Is the market growing, shrinking, or stable? Is it changing in other ways?
A declining market may be a good one to pull out of, or may present a terrific niche possibility. A growing market may be an opportunity for you to develop a growing niche. It could also present an enticing market to a large company which could swamp the market.

Market-share information is one of many factors involved in these kinds of strategic choice. You have to use your judgement. And remember that judgement based on facts beats guesswork.

Judgement based on facts beats guesswork.

Summary of Chapter 3

1. You have segmented your customer base (Figure 3.4).
2. You know (based on your research) why these people buy your products/services, and what needs or wants they satisfy.
3. This helps you to form a clear, easily communicated description of the target markets to which you can market effectively.
4. You can now set realistic target market objectives to include in your marketing plan, including the size of your markets,

your market-share goals, and other precise measures of performance. Fill in Figure 3.6.

Sample objectives might be to enter some niches, to try to attract certain market segments while dropping efforts to attract others, or to work on certain product lines that sell to current customers. You have to remember your own business situation and that these objectives are based on facts and analysis, not wishful thinking.

Figure 3.6   *Customer/Prospect summary form*

By:___GL_____   Date:__10/ 2 /89____

Reviewed by:_____   Date:_____

These are our most valuable customers and prospects, ranked from the top. (Make sure you list the market segments and their criteria.)

Name of customer   Market segment   Criteria (see Figure 3.3)

1. _ABC Co._   _40s, affluent, manufacturer, aggressive_
2. _DEF Co._   _40s, wealthy, service, aggressive_
3. _GHI Co_   _40s, wealthy, manufacturer, aggressive_
4. _____
5. _____

We should target these prospects:

Name of prospect   Market segment   Criteria (see Figure 3.3)

1. _XYZ Garage_   _Car_ ⎫ _Sales of £100,000⁺/yr_
2. _JML's Tyres_   _Car_ ⎬ _in business for at_
3. _Granite State Car Services car_ ⎭ _least 5 years_
4. _____
5. _____

We should consider these market niches:

1. Manufacturers of microwave components
2. Sporting goods retailers
3. Consultants and consulting companies
4. _____
5. _____

Our customer/prospect objectives for the next year are:

1. Penetrate car-related markets
2. Upgrade prospects/customers to £1,000,000 sale
3. Focus, Focus, Focus!

◀ CHAPTER 4 ▶
COMPETITIVE ANALYSIS

No business operates in a competitive vacuum, and there are plenty of other smart business owners looking to your target markets for their next sale.

In Chapter 1, Question 5, you made a list of obstacles which might stop you achieving your goals. One of the biggest impediments is the competition. No business operates in a competitive vacuum, and there are plenty of other business owners looking to your target markets for their next sale.

Business is competitive. Customers' needs and expectations shift. New products and different services fight for the consumers' money. New players enter the market while others leave it.

What can you do about competition? Plenty. Competitive analysis is an important part of your marketing plan. You can learn from your competitors and strengthen your business. You can predict their plans if you observe them closely. This takes work and close attention to detail. Most small business owners approach competitive analysis haphazardly. Set up a structured approach and seize a whopping competitive advantage.

Question 15: Who are your competitors?
Anyone who sells similar products/services in your marketplace, or similar products/services in other market-places, or who could sell similar products/services is a competitor. You compete for your target market's time and money. In the adver-

tising cliché, you want to gain their Attention, Interest, Desire and Action (the mnemonic is AIDA) – but so do a lot of competing businesses.

Competitive analysis begins with identifying your immediate competition. Who are your five leading competitors?

As you fine tune your analysis of the competition, you will want to add the less direct competition.

Future competitors may be the most threatening if you are in a highly desirable, rapidly growing market. But for most small business owners, just staying on top of the current market will be enough.

Remember, you aren't the only smart business owner out there. If you learn from your competitors, they can learn from you.

Figure 4.1 *Our competitors*

By: _GL_   Date: _11/2/89_

My closest competitors are:

1. _Bridge and Silverman_
2. _S, B; R_
3. _Purdy, Brown_
4. _____
5. _____

Other competitors (include potential as well as actual) are:

1. _Bigelow; Company_
2. _"Big-Eight" accounting firms_
3. _____

Business is competitive, and you have to profile the competition.

59

You have to learn a lot about your competition before you can make useful comparisons. Business is competitive, and you have to profile the competition. This may seem like spying. It is. A spy has to have some idea of his or her objectives. So do you. The information you gather should have a purpose and a structure that is updated periodically. This information sets your marketing strategies.

Use Figure 4.2, Competitor information, to organise your reports. Much of the information is readily available from Dun & Bradstreet and other reports. You can piece this information together yourself. Fill in these forms for each serious competitor, and keep the forms on file. Over a year or so you will develop a most informative dossier on your competition.

This is an area where knowledge is power. For many of us, the problem is gaining that knowledge. There are few short cuts, but the process is simple enough. You build the dossier piece by piece, over time, using the competition's advertising, press releases, promotional materials of all kinds, your own observations, and comments from vendors, customers, employees, friends, and your business advisers. As the file grows, you will know enough about your competitors to anticipate their moves, learn from their strengths and weaknesses, and increase your competitive advantage.

Don't feel badly about doing this. Your stronger competitors are doing this with you already.

Figure 4.2 *Competitor information*

Prepared by: _GL_____ Date: _11/2/89_____

Competitor: _S, B; R_____

Product/Service: _tax preparation + accounting services_

Location(s): _Portsmouth_____

Specific information:

Years in business:___**24**_____

Number of employees:__**20**_____

Value of sales:__**£ 3,000,000**_____

Unit sales:_____

Market share:__**approximately 20%**_____

Financial strength:__**excellent**_____

Profitability:__**?**_____

Players (include their age, experience in this business, training or education, strengths and weaknesses, and other pertinent information):

Chairman/owner:_____

Outside advisers:_____

Key employees:_____

The competition's marketing strategy:

Pricing:__**Accounting services: low   Taxes: high**__

Advertising themes:__**none**_____

Promotion/Public relations efforts:_____

Significant changes (new people, products, etc):_____

How this competitor competes with you:__**True conservative**____

Comments: **I need to do more research to finish this!**

Do your competitors see a weakness in your business or a market opportunity you have missed? Your top competitors look at your business for ideas; do the same to theirs. Your aim is to find out how you compare with your competition. What are their strengths relative to yours? Where do you differ?

Your top competitors look at your business for ideas. Do the same to theirs.

Many businesses go beyond profiling the competition. They have themselves 'shopped around' in order to have an unbiased appraisal of how they measure up against the competition.

Some questions you might want to raise are:

1. How are your competitors financed?
2. Can they raise more money? A division of a larger company, for example, has a potential advantage over a small business in this area.
3. Are they heavily in debt (which would make price competition dangerous to them)?
4. Are they investing in new products or services? Why?
5. What training do they give their personnel? Small business owners are notoriously unwilling to provide adequate training. This can be exploited.
6. What image (if any) are they trying to develop?
7. What are their target markets?
8. Do they compete on price, quality, service or convenience?

Question 16: What do your competitors do better than you?

Question 17: What do you do better than your competitors?
One application of Figure 4.2 is to alert you to your competitors' strengths and weaknesses compared with your business.

Perhaps they have a better product, a more motivated sales force, or better cost and quality controls which result in a price advantage. Perhaps they have a superior location or a better distribution system. Or perhaps they are instituting a strong sales training programme.

Once you know what their strengths are, learn from them. Avoid their weaknesses in your own business, but be ready to attack them with your marketing strategies. There is usually little difference between one small business and another. Those little differences, though, are what separate a profitable, enjoyable business from struggling businesses.

Use Figures 4.3 and 4.4 as guidelines.

In Figure 4.3, Comparing myself with my competitors, write down what your competition is doing in the five principal comparison areas. Then, in the last column, jot down how you compare in these areas.

Figure 4.3 *Comparing myself with my competitors*

Prepared by:___GL_____ Date:__11/2/89_____

Competitor:___5, B; R_____

	Describe your competitor's:	How do you compare?
Price	High	Lower, but rising
Quality	OK	Even better
Service	OK	" "
Location	Good	Poor — we're changing to a better one
Advertising	None	Aggressive
Other yardsticks	Been around a long time	Relatively new

The other yardsticks might be product lines, staffing, sales practices, or whatever you find to be important competitive information for your business. But you have to know how you compare on the other listed items, to differentiate your company from the competition.

All five major yardsticks are far more detailed than you may at first think. For example, consider advertising.

Look carefully at all the competitor's advertising. What are they trying to say? Do they feature price, delivery or reliability? Do they focus on one strength, for example, technical skill or convenience? How important do you think their advertised benefits are to the targeted market? Where do they advertise – trade journals? Radio or newspaper? Hoardings? Is their advertising more effective than yours? Should you re-evaluate your advertising?

Figure 4.4, Quick comparison, provides a list of comparisons based on what your customers are looking for. If you have been listening to your market, this form can provide valuable insights for your marketing strategies, and provide more ways to differentiate your business from the others.

Figure 4.4 *Quick comparison – benefits offered to our customers*

Your marketing strategy should be based on your strengths, the competition's weaknesses, and the market's needs and desires.

Competitor offers	We offer

Customer seeks:

Quality

Exclusivity

Lower prices ✓

Product line

Product service ✓ *Depends on size of account*

Reliability

Delivery ✓

Location ✓ *Town centre location*

Information ✓ *newsletter*

Availability ✓

Credit cards

Credit line

Guarantee ✓

Customer advice ✓

Accessories

Knowledgeability ✓

Polite help

Ours are lower than competition

More hand holding

Always meet deadlines
Easy access; will visit clients
news releases; seminars
Always when needed, including evenings; weekends

If not satisfied, client pays no fee
Always provided

Take courses every year

Your marketing strategy should be based on your strengths, the competition's weaknesses, and the market's needs and desires.

Strengthen weak areas in your business to become more competitive. This can pay off quickly. For example, if analysis shows

65

that you have unhelpful assistants and an untidy shop while the competitors have trained their people to be polite and provide a clean, well-lighted, spacious shop, your first move would be to ensure that you provide the same. The next step would be to advertise the change widely and build on whatever strengths you originally had.

Question 18: What is your competitive position?

Locate yourself on the competitive continuum in Figure 4.5. A visual reminder of where you are helps to stimulate and motivate your employees the same way that knowing your position in a league helps you to knuckle down to improve your own skills.

Figure 4.5   *Competitive continuum*

Strong_____+____|____–____Weak

Where are you located on this continuum? What are you going to do about it?

How do you rank compared with the competition in these areas? A plus means you are stronger than the competition, a minus means you are weaker.

	Strong	+		–	Weak
Finances				–	
Marketing				–	
Pricing		+			
Selling		+			
Production		+			
Distribution				–	
Training					
Personnel				–	

Summary of Chapter 4

1. You have identified your competition and have begun to collect detailed information on them (Figures 4.1 and 4.2).
2. You know your relative competitive position, based on a careful assessment of your leading competitors (Figure 4.5).
3. You know how you compare with the competition on some specific points, which helps to establish strategic directions on the 'build on your strengths and attack their weaknesses' principle (Figures 4.3 and 4.4).
4. This gives you the information to set realistic and attainable competitive objectives for the next year. Figure 4.6, Competitive objectives, summarises these goals. You will be referring back to Figure 4.6 in your marketing plan.

These objectives need not be detailed here. You will consider other aspects of your competitive position before writing your final marketing plan. While these preliminary objectives are very important as indicators for your planning, they will most likely be substantially modified by the time you flesh them out.

Figure 4.6 *Competitive objectives*

Prepared by:___G L_____   Date:__11/2/89_____

Reviewed by:_____   Date:_____

We need to improve our competitive position in these areas:

1. _Finances_____
2. _Marketing_____
3. _Training our personnel_____

We can build on our competitive strengths in these areas:

1. _Selling_____
2. _Production_____
3. _Personnel_____

We can attack our competition in their weak areas:

1. _Service_
2. _Offer business consulting in addition to_
   accounting services
3. _____

◀ CHAPTER 5 ▶

PRICE, LOCATION AND SALES PRACTICES

Three of the most important (and difficult to establish) pieces of your marketing plan are price (how to set prices to maximise profits and achieve other goals), location (where you do business, including distribution patterns), and sales practices (how you sell your products).

All pricing policies are competitive.

Within limits, these are fixed. Prices are somewhat determined by market conditions and competition. Where you open shop may already be established, but can be changed. Distribution patterns and delivery routes depend on sales patterns and customer demand. Sales practices are perhaps the hardest patterns to change, and cause the most problems.

However, you do have some latitude in each of these areas. You don't have to play follow-the-leader, or put up with an inadequate location or inept sales practices. You can change them to your benefit and competitive advantage.

Question 19: How do you establish prices?
The dilemma is whether to aim for high volume/low prices (the Woolworth route) or low volume/high prices (à la Aspreys).

This is complicated by the way your markets react to price

changes. Does a small price rise lead to a large drop in unit sales, or does a big price rise lead to a negligible drop in unit sales? This sensitivity to price changes is called 'price elasticity' and studies are often available through industry or trade associations. If your trade association doesn't have such studies, try sampling small segments of your markets. Your local college may be able to conduct an elasticity study for you, which has the additional benefit of shielding you from customers who may be highly price sensitive. Students conducting surveys can get away with more than you can in this delicate area.

Keep in mind that all pricing policies are competitive. Knowing how sensitive your target markets are to price change puts you at an advantage over firms which follow a reactive pricing policy, but there are many other factors to keep in mind.

To set your pricing policy, follow these five steps:

1. *Define your pricing objectives.* Tie these to your overall marketing and business goals (see Figures 1.3 and 1.5).

Some common pricing objectives include maintaining or building market share, maximising profits or return on investment, meeting competition, introducing new products, increasing sales, or all of these.

Knowledge beats guesswork every time.

Figure 5.1 *Pricing factors*

PRICE = Image + Service + Product + Overhead + Profit

Pricing policies are influenced by:
1. *Price sensitivity* (elasticity).
2. *Quality.* High quality and high prices often go together.
3. *Product differentiation.* High differentiation and high prices, and low differentiation (commodity products) and low prices, often go together.
4. *Competition.* Competitive markets and price chopping as a market-share strategy go together.

5. *Service.* The more service you provide, the higher the price. A fully assembled, carefully chosen bicycle from a cycle shop costs more than the same bike bought disassembled from a warehouse.

6. *Location.* City centre stores command higher prices than those located in local shopping malls.

7. *Target markets.* Some markets buy on price. A low price can scare people off ('The price is so low – what's wrong with this?') or be an excellent marketing tool. Know your markets.

8. *Marketing objectives.* Are you looking for market share? Profits? New markets? Your objectives must be reflected in your price strategies.

9. *Your business costs.* Your pricing has to reflect your business, not someone else's.

Perceived value to customers = Product + Intangibles (service, quality are examples) + Specialised expertise

---

2. *Establish price ranges.* This is complicated, so call in your accountant or financial advisers. Three questions to raise when setting price ranges are:

☐ *What is your break-even point?* (See Figure 5.2.) This establishes the low end of the acceptable range. You must at least meet your expenses (break-even) before you can make a profit. Can you reach break-even given sales forecasts and current prices? How far can you exceed it?

☐ *What are your profit goals?* If you can't reach the profit goals given unit sales forecasts and acceptable prices, you might want to rethink your strategies, or market more aggressively. (See Figures 1.5 and 2.9.)

☐ *How do your target markets perceive your products/services?* This includes questions of price sensitivity as well as product differentiation. Oddly enough, the small business scourge 'lack of courage in pricing' often stems from not knowing how the market perceives the value of products and services. Don't guess here. Use surveys, questionnaires, market research, and trade studies. Knowledge beats guesswork every time. This piece of knowledge helps you to establish the upper limit of your price range. Sometimes this is called 'what the traffic will bear'.

Fill in Figure 5.3 for each product/service or each product/service line. Save these forms for future review.

Figure 5.2 *Break-even analysis*

Break-even analysis pinpoints where revenue equals total costs. To calculate your break-even point, take your most recent profit and loss account and identify each cost as either fixed or variable. Fixed costs are independent of sales level, while variable costs rise and fall with sales. Mixed costs involve elements of both. Most costs will fall readily into fixed or variable. For those that don't, allocate 50 per cent to fixed costs, and 50 per cent to variable.

Fixed Expenses:	Variable Expenses:
Salaries	Sales commissions
National insurance	Boxes, paper, etc
Rent	Travel
Rates/community tax	Freight
Benefits	Overtime
Utilities	Bad debts
Licences and fees	
Insurance	Mixed:
Advertising	Telephone
Legal and accounting	Postage
Depreciation	
Interest	
Maintenance and cleaning	

The break-even formula is:

$$BE = F/(S-V)$$

where BE = break-even sales in pounds
  F = fixed costs in pounds
  S = sales expressed as 100 per cent
  V = variable costs as a percentage of sales

If F = £10,000, S = 100 per cent, and V = 50 per cent, then BE = (£10,000/50%) = £20,000.

In other words, costs will exceed revenue until you have sold £20,000 worth of goods.

Figure 5.3 *Price range guidelines*

By: **GL** Date: **12/2/89**

Product/Service: **All accounting services**

Price range: £ **40/hr** to £ **75/hr**

1. Price floor:

    (a) Mark-up (gross margin) is _____% of retail price.
    (b) Manufacturer's suggested price is £_____.
    (c) Fixed costs are £_____. Variable costs are £_____ or _____% of sales.
    (d) Break-even is £_____.

2. Special considerations for this product's price are:

    ☑ Service
    ☐ Status
    ☑ Quality
    ☐ Loss leader
    ☐ Demand
    ☐ Product life
    ☐ Overhead
    ☐ Downtime
    ☐ Competition
    ☐ Market penetration costs
    ☐ Other (specify):

    something to think about: Our fees can be higher if the clients' perception of value is raised!

3. Turnover rate is _____ times per year. **not applicable**

4. Industry turn average is _____ times per year. **"**

5. Going rate is **£50 to £100/hr**

6. I estimate _____ units will be sold. not applicable

7. _31_ (~~number of units~~) hours/week at £_75/hr_ will cover my fixed costs.

8. Top price possible is £_____. (This estimate is based on the customer's perception of value.)

Comments:

_____

_____

Your price strategies have to reflect your business's cost structures and profit goals, not someone else's.

3. *Define competitive pricing strategy.* See Figure 5.4 for some ideas. Since all pricing strategies are competitive, a major factor in your choice will be what the others are doing. This doesn't mean that you want to follow them. It does mean that you want to know what they are doing so you can defeat them in the market-place.

Figure 5.4 *Price setting considerations*

Consider setting prices above your competitor's prices if:
- ☐ Your market is not sensitive to price changes.
- ☐ Your market consists mainly of growing businesses.
- ☐ Your product is an integral part of an established system.
- ☐ Your reputation for status, service, and other positive perceptions in the market increases your products' perceived value.
- ☐ Your customers can easily build your price into their selling price.
- ☐ Your product is only a tiny percentage of your customers' total costs.

Consider setting your prices just below your competition if:
- ☐ Your market is sensitive to price changes.
- ☐ You're attempting to enter a new market.
- ☐ Your customers need to reorder parts or supplies.
- ☐ Your business is small enough for a lower price not to cause your larger competitors to start a price war.
- ☐ You have the option of economical production or purchasing which decreases your unit cost.
- ☐ You have not reached full production capacity.

4. *Consider the impact of product lines, inventory costs, and selling costs.* Sometimes you have to flesh out a product line to meet other competitive pressures and rather than carry the product forever, you decide to sell it off even at a loss. Inventory costs are a hidden burden on many retail businesses (ask your accountant) and can drive up your short-term borrowing needs.

Some businesses find that sales costs are the dominant pricing factor. Think of encyclopedia sales, where everyone from the door-to-door salesperson on gets a commission. The £600 price is based on a minimal product cost, plus a substantial research and development cost, plus a staggering sales cost.

Keep your costs in mind when setting prices. Your price strategies have to reflect your business's cost structures and profit goals, not someone else's.

5. *Choose a flexible pricing strategy.* Every industry has its own favourite pricing strategy, and you should use your industry pattern as a guide.

The four main methods of setting prices are:

☐ *Suggested or going rate.* This is the least defensible method, since it removes your business from the pricing decision. This is far and away the most common method. It is simple. It makes no work. It also is almost totally ineffective.

☐ *Full-cost pricing.* If you can identify all your operating costs, then distribute them over merchandise costs, add a preset profit, and crank out the prices. One weakness of this method is that the merchandise has to be sold, and in sufficient quantities to push you past the break-even point. Another more glaring weakness is that full-cost pricing presupposes that your accounting system is able to capture all the costs and make accurate forecasts.

Set firm price ranges for each product/ service or product/ service line, keep an eye open for competitive moves, and check constantly to ensure that your prices serve your profit and other marketing objectives.

The advantage is that full-cost pricing makes pricing simple. It is most helpful as a guideline, and can help narrow the price ranges set earlier.

☐ *Gross margin.* This can be worked out either as a mark-up (adding a percentage of wholesale cost to your base cost) or as a mark-on (percentage of the retail price represented by the gross margin).

This method takes operating costs and market factors into account, but is only as good as your ability to meet projected sales levels. The big advantage is that gross margin pricing helps to set uniform price floors. You can then change prices to reflect market conditions, the market's sensitivity to price change, competition and so on.

☐ *Flexible mark-ups.* This is less rigid than full-costing, and is particularly helpful during periods of fluctuating prices. It demands that you have information about your market's sensitivity to price changes.

The main weakness of this approach is that it is all too easy to pursue sales at the expense of profit. While you don't want to hold on to inventory too long, you don't want to give it away either. This is a problem most merchants have to grapple with.

The best method of all is to combine the strengths of these four methods. Set firm price ranges for each product/service or product/service line, keep an eye open for competitive moves, and check constantly to ensure that your prices serve your profit and other marketing objectives. Whatever you do, don't slap a price on your products and refuse to change it when conditions change. Rigidity is as great a danger as being totally reactive to every market whim.

Try to ascertain factual answers to the questions in Figure 5.5 when you set pricing policies.

Figure 5.5 *Pricing checklist*

Estimating demand:
1. Which products/services do customers shop around for?
2. Which products/services are in greater demand even at higher prices?
3. Are certain products/services in greater demand at one time of the year than another? If so, which? And what is the duration of that demand?
4. Do your customers expect a certain price range?
5. What is the balance between price and quality in your market?

The competition:
1. What are your competitors' pricing strategies?
2. Are your prices based on an average gross margin which is consistent with your competitors'?
3. Is your policy to sell consistently at a higher price, lower price, or at the same price as your competitors? Why?
4. How do your competitors respond to your prices?

Pricing and market share:
1. What is your present market share?
2. What are your market share goals? To increase share? Maintain share?
3. What effect will price changes have on your market share?
4. Is your production capacity consistent with your market-share goals?

Strategy:
1. Have you found out how pricing affects your sales/volume goals?
2. How can pricing help you to gain new business?
3. Have you tested the impact of price strategies on your markets?
4. Are your strategies in line with broader economic trends?

Policies:
1. How does the nature of your products affect their price?
2. How does your method of distribution affect price?
3. Do your promotional policies affect prices?

The three most important factors in retail business are location, location and location.

Question 20: How does your location affect you?

According to a number of studies, the most common reason to pick a new business site is 'noticed vacancy'. Since the three most important factors in retail business are location, location and location, it is no surprise that many small businesses never reach their full potential.

If you are already in business, you still have to keep track of your trading area. Perhaps you're considering a move to a new location, or building a branch office. New roads are constructed. Populations shift, town planning requirements are altered, competitors come and go. If you can identify the advantages and disadvantages of your location, you can do something about them.

The marketing challenge is: how do you evaluate the strengths and weaknesses of your location (actual or proposed)? While some businesses don't have to worry much about location, most do. If location is important to you, get answers to these four questions:

1. *What is the traffic flow at the site?* Exposure to pedestrian and vehicle traffic will affect sales and advertising. See Figure 5.6 for some ideas.

Figure 5.6 *Traffic counts*

You need two traffic counts, one for pedestrians and one for vehicles. You should find out:

- ☐ How many people pass by during your business hours
- ☐ When they pass by
- ☐ Who these people are
- ☐ Where they are from
- ☐ What their shopping plans might be
- ☐ How many are logical prospects for your products or services
- ☐ If there are seasonal or other predictable fluctuations
- ☐ Where they currently buy your kind of products or services.

These pieces of information help you to evaluate your site. Your advertising and other promotional programmes need this information too.

---

2. *What are the other shops or offices in the area?* Complementary businesses help. It's no accident that there are clusters of shops in almost every city. Fast food restaurants, and department stores are two such clusters. Shopping malls are ideal for some businesses; others prefer stand-alone sites.

Unless you have very good reasons to do otherwise, find out where businesses similar to yours tend to be located and join the trend. Trade associations, industry publications, and your own observations can help here.

Transitional areas pose a special opportunity and challenge. In many cities, for example, the centres are coming back after years of blight. Ask the local estate agents, your Chamber of Commerce, bankers, local government officials, and regional planners what's happening. They all will have good ideas and suggestions for you to evaluate and perhaps act on.

3. *How's the parking?* Is the site easily accessible? Safe? Convenient? Unless you have a location where parking is of no concern, this is a big question. It doesn't matter what the traffic count is if people can't find close, adequate, safe parking.

4. *What costs are involved?* Rent = Space Costs + Advertising. A poor location will compel you to spend more on advertising, while a good location allows you to spend less. As examples, shopping centre rents are high, but the traffic flow in a good one justifies the cost. A low rent, while appealing, will be offset by increased advertising costs. The totals may be the same.

A poor location will compel you to spend more on advertising, while a good location allows you to spend less.

Figure 5.7 *Site evaluation*

By: _GL_   Date: _15/2/89_

1. How ~~will~~ *does* the site affect your business? Not much – our business is generated by word-of-mouth and ads

2. How does the appearance of the building affect your business? It's all right – successful + professional looking + not too plush

3. Does the shop's or office's appearance complement your business's image? It doesn't hurt.

4. Do you (or can you) use the location to your best advantage? How? Our office is easy to find.

5. Should you move or consider moving? Why? Not yet

6. Is the neighbourhood changing? If so, how? How will it affect your business? Yes – businesses and the local economy are growing.

7. Is the site high- or low-rent? Moderate.

8. Is the rent competitive for the area? yes

9. If your site is low-rent, how will you attract customers?

10. Is the location good from a competitive viewpoint? Satisfactory – maybe we should think about moving nearer the centre?

11. Is the traffic sufficient for your sales objectives? Not applicable

12. Will neighbouring shops help to draw customers? " "

13. Is parking adequate? Would paying for customer parking make sense? yes

14. Can you develop additional traffic? How? not applicable

15. What disadvantages does the site have? How will you overcome them? None

16. Is this the best site available for your business? If no, why not? It's adequate for now

Question 21: What are your sales practices?
Don't assume that your current method is the only way you can sell product/service.

Examining and improving selling methods is part of your marketing plan.

Examining and improving selling methods is part of your marketing plan.

1. *How are you currently selling your products/services?* For example, a mortgage broker, might sell solely by referral from an estate agent or by word of mouth – or through more assertive methods. Most shops rely on location plus advertising in local media.

You might be able to add sales through direct mail or using sales representatives. What changes might result in more sales? Are you cross-selling to your current customers or merely taking orders?

2. *What are your competitors' selling practices?* If they are adding salespeople, or changing their advertising strategies, or moving to a new location, better take note. How do they get new customers and retain old ones?

Check on the competition, either in person or by using a consultant who will provide a detailed analysis of their sales methods. While you're at it, have your own business checked too. Close to 75 per cent of lost customers complain of rude, discourteous or poorly informed salespersons – and the irate customer complains to an average of 11 other people. That's powerful negative word-of-mouth.

3. *What follow-up do you have after the sale?* Your best prospects are your current customers. If you don't provide adequate service after the sale, each customer will end up buying from your competition.

If you never have repeat customers as part of your marketing strategy, fine. But for 99 per cent of businesses, repeat sales are vitally important (and frequently overlooked in the scramble for new customers). Since you buy customers with your advertising and promotion efforts as well as with your products and services, it makes sense to hang on to them as long as possible.

How should you follow up? Direct mail is excellent and can be low cost. Phone calls are good. Maintain a customer service desk or a call-in number. Set a strong returns policy favourable to the customer.

Follow-up differentiates your business from all the others. Satisfied customers talk. So do unhappy customers. Think of the effort BMW puts into its service department. Think of how a good car dealer provides after-sales service.

4. *What kind of sales training do you provide?* Salespeople aren't born knowing how to sell, and while you may be able to impart all the product knowledge they need, sales training is a highly specialised field.

If you don't provide sales training, why not? If it's on the grounds that sales training is an expense that you'd rather not incur, you can count on being swamped by your competitors.

Figure 5.8   *Checking on the competition*

By:___GL_____   Date:__15/2/89____

Competitor:___5, B, R_____

Location:___Portsmouth_____

Rate 1 (poor) to 5 (excellent)   **Rating**   **Comments**

1. Appearance and design of store   *5*

2. Employees' characteristics:

    A. Telephone manners   *4*

	Rating	Comments
B. Courtesy	4	They've been
C. Helpfulness	4	around for
D. Appearance	5	a long time,
E. Product knowledge	4	and are
F. Ability to handle complaints	3	well known.
G. Ability to cross-sell	4	Also, they
3. Availability of products	4	have a very
4. Convenience of location	5	good location
5. Added services (delivery, etc)	4	
6. Other (specify):		

Summary of Chapter 5

1. Pricing objectives are set, and a pricing policy that serves the sales, profit and marketing goals of your company has been considered.
2. Your location has been analysed (Figure 5.7).
3. Sales practices – including training – have been examined, and your competitors checked to ascertain their sales strengths and weaknesses (Figure 5.8).

Figure 5.9 *Pricing objectives*

By: __GL_____   Date: __15/2/89____

Product/Service: __Explanation of Client's financial statements__

Refer to Figures 5.3, 5.4, and 5.5, and fill in one of these forms for each product/service.

My pricing objectives are	This objective will accomplish	My time frame for reaching this objective is
1. To charge an average £200-300/mth	A 'door opener' for more business	Right now
2.		
3.		
4.		
5.		

Figure 5.10 *How can you improve your company's sales practices?*

By: **GL**   Date: **15/2/89**

Product/Service: **All accounting services**

My sales practice objectives are	This objective will accomplish	My time frame for reaching this objective is
1. Focus on the car industry	make us experts for that trade; we'll get referrals, too	1 year
2. Develop local market	save us time on the road	Right now
3. Attend sales training programme	Improve our stocks	6 months
4.		

◀ CHAPTER 6 ▶

STRENGTHS AND WEAKNESSES

Your marketing strategy has to reflect the strengths and weaknesses of your business. This includes the competitive strengths and weaknesses noted in Chapter 4.

In a successful business, all important parts of running the business are covered adequately if not necessarily brilliantly. No major area can be left unattended. A management audit (see Figures 6.1 and 6.2) helps you to gauge the quality of your management, spot areas where improvement is needed, and makes sure that there are no glaring omissions to trip you up.

Your aim is to establish the right balance for your business. Your business is an assembly of systems, each of which has to work well for the whole business to be profitable. The audit helps to make sure that your business has all its necessary parts, that they are all working together towards the same goals, and that the goals are suitable for the resources of your business.

Furthermore, all parts should be the right size. A small business danger is letting one part outgrow the rest, which leads to an unbalanced allocation of resources. As you conduct your management audit, which should take only an hour or so to complete, keep balance in mind.

Your marketing strategy has to reflect the strengths and weaknesses of your business.

Any item which is ticked 'No' warrants your immediate attention since it flags a weakness in your business. While a 'Yes' answer affirms that the area in question is at least covered, there could still be room for improvement. You may want to go over Figure 6.1 again looking for 'Yes' areas that you can improve on. Remember, build on strengths, shore up weaknesses.

Figure 6.1 *Management audit*

By:___GL___ Date:___19/2/89___

Based upon my analysis of the business, I believe that the operation is being run satisfactorily in:

	Yes	No
1. Sales and marketing		
A. Pricing		
Are prices in line with current industry practice?	✓	
Is your pricing policy based on your cost structure?	✓	
Have you conducted price sensitivity studies?		✓
B. Market research		
Have you identified target markets?	✓ (some)	
Do you segment your markets?		✓
Have you identified customer wants/needs?		✓
Do you know how your markets perceive your products/services?		✓
Has your business taken advantage of market potential?	✓	
Has the competition been analysed?	✓	
C. Personal selling		
Are your sales practices satisfactory?	✓	
D. Customer service		
Is customer service a priority?	✓	
Is there a rational balance between serving your customers' needs and good business practice?	✓ (most of the time)	
E. Advertising and public relations		
Do you select media for measurable results?	✓ (not always)	

	Yes	No
Is your advertising consistent?		✓
Does your advertising budget make sense in terms of the level of business and its anticipated, planned growth?		✓

(only in yellow pages)

F. Sales management

	Yes	No
Are sales people and outside agents properly directed in their duties?	✓	
Do you establish individual sales goals?	✓	
Do you provide adequate sales support?		✓
Are your sales people trained?		✓

G. Market planning

	Yes	No
Do you have a marketing budget?		✓
Do you have a market plan?		✓
Has your business taken advantage of market opportunities?		✓

2. Business operations

A. Purchasing

	Yes	No
Are reputable, competitive vendors used?	*NA*	
Do you have a purchasing programme?	*NA*	

B. Stock control

	Yes	No
Do you know what your stock turn is?		
Is slow-moving stock managed?	*NA*	
Have you established rational reordering policies?		

C. Scheduling

	Yes	No
Do goods and materials move through the business without hang-ups and problems?	✓ *(usually)*	
Do you know how long each job should take?	✓	

D. Quality control

	Yes	No
Are inferior incoming materials returned to vendors?		
Are reject rates minimised?		
Do you have a 'do it right the first time' policy?	✓	

E. Business growth

	Yes	No
Has your business grown at least above the rate of inflation?	✓	
Have you met your asset growth, sales, and profit goals?		

* we didn't have goals — and need them!

	Yes	No

F. Site location
   Do you have the right business location? ✓

G. Insurance
   Do you have an annual insurance review? ✓ (No)
   Are the proper risks to your business (and to yourself) covered? ✓ (No)
   Do you put your insurance package out to tender every year? ✓ (No)

3. **Financial**
   A. Bookkeeping and accounting
      Are your books adequate? ✓ (Yes)
      Are records easy to come by? ✓ (Yes)
      Can you get information when you need it? ✓ (Yes)
      Do you have monthly profit and loss accounts? ✓ (Yes)
      Do you have annual financial statements? ✓ (Yes)

   B. Budgeting
      Do you use a cash flow budget? ✓ (Yes)
      Do you use variance analysis monthly? ✓ (Yes)
      Are capital equipment purchases budgeted? ✓ (Yes)

   C. Cost control
      Are cost items managed? ✓ (Yes)
      Are high cost items treated separately?
      Is the budget used as the primary cost control tool? ✓ (No)

   D. Raising money
      Have you been successful in raising capital when it was needed? ✓ (Yes)

   E. Credit and collection
      Do you know your C&C costs? ✓ (No)
      Is your current policy successful? ✓ (No)
      Do you review C&C policies regularly? ✓ (Yes)
      Do you have a management policy on debtors? ✓ (Yes)

	Yes	No

F. Dealing with banks
    Is your relationship with your bank open and friendly? ✔
    Do you have access to more than one source of financing? ✔

G. Cost of money
    Do you compare the cost of money (interest) with your profit ratios? ✔
    Are interest rates and loan conditions appropriate? ✔

H. Specific tools
    Do you know and use:
    1. Break-even analysis? ✔
    2. Cash flow projections and analysis? ✔
    3. Monthly profit and loss accounts? ✔
    4. Balance sheets? ✔
    5. Ratio analysis? ✔
    6. Industry operating ratios? ✔
    7. Tax planning? ✔

4. **Personnel**
    A. Hiring
        Has the right mix of people been employed? ✔ (No)
        Do you recruit from a pool of qualified applicants? ✔
        Do you maintain a file of qualified applicants? ✔

    B. Training
        Are your employees suitably trained for their jobs? ✔

    C. Motivating
        Do your employees appear to enjoy what they are doing? ✔ *(not all the time)*

    D. Enforcing policies
        Does there seem to be logic and order to what goes on in the business? ✔
        Are reviews and evaluations performed on schedule? ✔ (No)

    E. Communicating
        Are people informed and brought in on decisions? ✔
        Do you create opportunities for employees to set their own goals? ✔

	Yes	No

5. **Administrative management**
   A. Record keeping
   Are records of past transactions and events easy to find? ✓
   Are records retained for at least the minimum legal period? ✓
   Is access to personnel files limited? ✓ (No)

   B. Problem solving
   Are there few unresolved problems? ✓

   C. Decision making
   Are you decisive? ✓
   Is there a chain of command? ✓

   D. Government regulations
   Are you aware of local and government regulations that affect your business? ✓

   E. Leadership
   Do you actually take charge of the business and its employees? ✓

   F. Developing subordinates
   If you were to die or suddenly become disabled, is there a ready successor? ✓

   G. Business law
   Do you have a working knowledge of applicable business law regarding contracts, agencies, sale of goods, and so on? ✓
   Do you know how current contracts and other legal obligations affect your business? ✓

   H. Dealing with professionals
   Do you have and use an accountant, solicitor, and business consultant? ✓
   Do you use outside advisers? ✓

Figure 6.2 *Good management scorecard*

	Yes	No
1. We operate with a complete and up-to-date business plan which includes:		
A. One-year and three-year projections		✓
B. A capital budget		✓
2. We operate with an annual marketing plan which includes:		
A. Specific sales and profit goals, and timetables	✓	
B. Strategies and tactics for the next three years		✓
C. Budgets, forecasts and benchmarks	✓	
D. A sales plan	✓	
Our marketing plan also includes:		
E. The demographics of our target markets		✓
F. A well thought out definition of the markets we serve	✓	
G. A definition of the needs/wants our products and services fill	✓	
H. An analysis of the growth potential of our markets	✓	
I. A competitive analysis		✓
J. A definition of our 'Unique Selling Proposition'		✓
K. Projections for other products or services that could be developed	✓	
L. Timetables for research and development		✓
3. We use monthly budgets and statements which include:		
A. Thorough and up-to-date records	✓	
B. Cash flow budget	✓	
C. Profit and loss account	✓	
D. Balance sheet	✓	
E. Variance analysis	✓	
F. Ratio analysis	✓	
G. Standard cost comparisons		✓
H. Cash reconciliation	✓	
4. We have developed an information base that allows us to:		
A. Keep track of new developments in the industry	✓	
B. Obtain and study key trade information	✓	
C. Understand what 'state of the art' means in this business		✓
D. Provide customers with the best available information pertaining to our products and services	✓	
E. Keep all our employees adequately informed	✓	

	Yes	No

5. I'm certain that the business is properly capitalised since I:
A. Base capitalisation on worst-case planning   ✓ (No)
B. Have emergency funds (or access to them)   ✓ (No)
C. Have discussed this with my bank   ✓ (No)

6. I understand the value of the business because I've made use of:
A. Professional appraisers   ✓ (No)
B. Present-value methods to evaluate terms   ✓ (No)
C. Professional tax planning advice   ✓ (No)
D. Accurate, timely financial information   ✓ (Yes)

7. We strive to improve production, quality and operations by:
A. Keeping the plant in top condition   ✓ (No)
B. Maintaining safe conditions   ✓ (Yes)
C. Establishing high standards   ✓ (Yes)
D. Standing behind our products/services   ✓ (Yes)
E. Not tolerating shoddy performance   ✓ (Yes)
F. Working for consistency   ✓ (Yes)
G. Using our company's 'look' as a statement to our markets   ✓ (Yes)

8. Our personnel decisions are based on humane, carefully considered policies which include:
A. Checklists to make sure objectives are clear   ✓ (No)
B. Communication to make sure objectives are understood   ✓ (No)
C. Written job descriptions   ✓ (No)
D. Regular progress and performance evaluations   ✓ (No)
E. Fair recruitment practices   ✓ (Yes)
F. Fair wage scales   ✓ (Yes)

	Yes	No

9. As for my own managerial skills, I work hard to:

	Yes	No
A. Develop my problem-solving abilities	✓	
B. Stay calm always		✓
C. Be objective		✓
D. Avoid investments in my own ego	✓	
E. Listen to my employees	✓	
F. Plan changes in our course to minimise negative effects	✓	
G. Make decisions promptly	✓	
H. Get the facts behind problems always		✓
I. Accept my own limitations	✓	
J. Delegate tasks that can be done more efficiently by someone else	✓	
K. Analyse all available options		✓
L. Develop my reading/study habits	✓	
M. Improve my skills	✓	
N. Consider and evaluate risks	✓	
O. Be positive with customers, employees, and associates	✓	

Once more, 'No' answers are red flags. 'Yes' answers indicate acceptable levels, but may offer ideas for improved performance.

The next step is to relate your findings directly to your marketing plans. 'No' answers to any item in Figure 6.1 or 6.2 are weaknesses that have to be acknowledged and dealt with. Those 'Yes' answers that identify areas of particular strength should also be noted; they are strengths to build on.

Your search for strengths and weaknesses goes further. Some areas of strength or weakness are outside your business. Others are internal, but not captured in the checklists above.

Question 22: What is your business strong at?

Advantages may be things like an outstanding product, skilled personnel, superb location, close relationship with an advertising agency, or outstanding technology. You want to find as many of these as possible to help you to define your marketing niche more sharply.

If you can predict external weaknesses, you gain a major competitive advantage over the unprepared competitor.

External strengths include a number of factors you have little control over. For instance, your competition may be feeble, or your market expanding, or the local economy booming. These advantages tend to be temporary. No economy booms forever, markets have limits, and weak competition opens the doors for stronger competitors. Still, you want to be aware of and carefully monitor external advantages so you can benefit from them.

Question 23: What is your business weak at?

Samples of internal weaknesses include ineffective, untrained or underused personnel, lack of sales support materials, frequent stock-outs, poor quality, and undercapitalisation. While some of these may have to be addressed from a company-wide point of view, some are essentially marketing problems. Do you have a marketing budget? If not, why not? Do you have sales training? If not, why not? Are sales support systems weak? Then strengthen them.

Your awareness and understanding of external problems and weaknesses help you to handle them. Perhaps you face new, aggressive competition, or the local economy is taking a nosedive, or your market is evaporating owing to a new technology. You have to know what these larger forces are and how your business might respond to them. You may not be able to control them, but you *can* control how your business reacts. If you can predict external weaknesses, you gain a major competitive advantage over the unprepared competitor. He gets swamped while you ride the wave.

List the strengths and weaknesses, both internal and external, that come to mind on Figure 6.3. Add those discovered in Figures 6.1 and 6.2. Then go out and look for more. This is an open-ended process which will become second nature. As you identify the strengths and weaknesses, ask yourself:

1. Can I change this circumstance?
2. Can I take advantage of or build on this?

3. If it is beyond my control, how does it or will it affect my business?
4. How long will these advantages and disadvantages last – and how can my business take advantage of these circumstances?

Figure 6.3 *Strengths and weaknesses*

By: _RM & GL_   Date: _19/2/89_

List your business's strengths and weaknesses. Use Figures 6.1 and 6.2 as guides. Give very brief descriptions and categorise each as 'internal' or 'external' by ticking the appropriate column.

Strengths	Internal	External
1. Customer service	✓	
2. Financial management	✓	
3. Bank relations	✓	✓
4. Quality of service	✓	
5.		

Weaknesses		
1. Advertising + PR	✓	
2. Market planning	✓	
3. Pricing	maybe!	
4. Insurance	✓	
5. Capitalisation	✓	

The final step in this process is to review Figure 6.3 and rank the strengths and weaknesses. Since they represent significant opportunities and problems, you want to work on the most important first.

Figure 6.4 *Analysis of a specific strength or weakness*

Fill in one of these forms for each strength or weakness.

By: __GL_____ Date: __20/2/89____

Describe the strength or weakness. Be as factual as possible.

_Customer service is a strength. We provide tax
news and other information in our newsletter. We
always meet deadlines & are always accessible—
not just from 9 to 5._

What are the probable results of this strength or weakness?

_We have loyal clients and close customer
relations_

What should I do to capitalise on or correct this?

_Promote word-of-mouth PR in our ads. Also, use
endorsements. Perhaps we should use this approach
to get our clients' help: "We have a problem
and we need your help"_

Set dates for implementation and review.

_Within month — we will talk to 5 clients
and aim to get 20 referrals._

Summary of Chapter 6

1. Two management audits have been conducted (Figures 6.1 and 6.2) to discover internal strengths and weaknesses. After studying them, the more important strengths and weaknesses have been listed on Figure 6.3.
2. Other strengths and weaknesses have been considered, and added to Figure 6.3.
3. These were then ranked in order of importance, and some of them singled out for immediate attention using Figure 6.4.
4. Strengths and weaknesses help you or hinder you according to your awareness of them. If you are not reaching your sales and marketing goals, or if you think the goals should be higher, read this chapter again.

◀ CHAPTER 7 ▶

ADVERTISING AND PROMOTION

Figure 7.1   *Promotion audit*

By: __GL__   Date: __21/2/89__

Do you: Yes   No

Know where new business is coming from?   ✓

Keep track of referrals and thank the sources?   ✓

Track advertising and direct mail responses?   ✓ (we need to do more!)

Spend advertising budgets in proportion to
  your product mix?   ✓

Project a strong, consistent image in all
  materials, livery, stationery and so forth?   ✓ (needs to be stronger)

Have a professionally designed logo?   ✓

Sell benefits to customers in all promotional
  material?   ✓

Know what has worked, what has not worked
  and why?   ✓

Have a yearly advertising, public relations and
  promotion plan?   ✓

Involve your entire staff in the promotional
  process?   ✓

Advertise to your staff as well as to your markets?	_____	✔ (not enough)
Have strong relationships with media people and advertising professionals in your community?	_____	✔
Assign one person to make sure your plan is implemented?	_____	✔
Have a professionally designed 'facilities brochure' which explains who and what your business is?	_____	✔
Follow up promotional efforts with selling on other items (if appropriate)?	✔	_____
Have professional window and point-of-sale displays?	_____	✔
Analyse your probable competition in connection with the direct and indirect sales promotional methods you plan to use?	_____	✔

For any 'No' answer, you have another reason to use a professional advertising/public relations/promotion agency.

Advertising and promotion are not substitutes for selling. They can make prospects aware of you, make them receptive to your products and services, even stir them to call or write for more information. But they can't replace continual sales efforts.

Advertising and promotion can't replace ongoing sales efforts.

You have already done most of the groundwork for your advertising campaigns and other promotions. Effective creativity is based on thorough knowledge of products, target markets, and competitive conditions. Your advertising agency has to know what your objectives are, what your budget is, and when you plan to run your campaign.

Figure 7.2 *Advertising base*

A successful promotional campaign requires answers to these questions.

1. *Who?* Who are your customers and prospects? You have already segmented your markets, so you can describe who the promotion is aimed at. See Figure 3.4.
2. *Why?* What are you trying to accomplish? Increase sales? Introduce a new product? Retain or increase market share? Create or maintain an image? See Question 25 in this chapter.
3. *When?* Timing in advertising is all-important. The best promotion will fail if the timing is off.
4. *What?* What specific products or services are you trying to move? What is their unique selling proposition?
5. *Where?* What media would be best for your campaign?
6. *How?* Leave this one to your advertising agency. You have enough to do running your business. You have to review and approve the campaign.

The details – the 'where' and 'how' – are less important than getting your message out. Your advertising agency will save a lot of time here, help you to make the right choices, and meet the deadlines. Many good campaigns are sabotaged by well-intentioned business owners who know a lot about their business but little about advertising and promotion. Unfortunately, everyone thinks he or she is a good copywriter and art director. Nothing could be further from the truth.

Advertising and promotion have to be managed the same way as you manage other parts of your business. You have to know what resources you can afford to commit to them (Question 24), what you want to accomplish (Question 25), and form a coherent strategy that ties in with your broader business and marketing goals (Question 26).

To illustrate the complexity of the problem, look at the promotional methods in Figure 7.3. Your promotional mix will employ several of these, plus others that aren't listed.

Figure 7.3 *Promotion smorgasbord*

Promotion encompasses a wide range of activities:

Paid advertising

Radio
Television
Print
    Newspapers
    Magazines
    Free or classified ad magazines
✓ Yellow Pages
    Special directories (regional, seasonal, Chamber of Commerce)
    Trade or industry directories
    Cooperative or 'co-op' ad support from your vendors
    Outdoor hoardings

Direct mail
    Letters
✓ Newsletters
    Sales or product/service announcements
✓ Flyers
    Postcards
    'Special customer' offers
    Brochures
    Direct response
    Coupons

Public relations
✓ News releases
    Articles in magazines, journals, etc *we should do more of these!*
✓ Speaking engagements
✓ Interviews
    Sponsorship of community events and activities
✓ Seminars
✓ Workshops
    Club memberships

Telemarketing
    Enquiry handling
✓ Direct marketing by phone
    Service: customer complaints, follow-up, special offers

Selling on
✓ Presentation materials *we need these*
✓ Personal letters

✓ Customised proposals
✓ Some telemarketing
Sales personnel training *We need this too*

Sales promotions
    Discounts ✓ *½ hour free consultation*
    Loss leaders
    Coupons
    'Buy one, get one free'

Special advertising
    Book matches, key chains and other novelties
    Calendars
    Diaries

we could have coffee mugs with our name and phone number on them.

Facilities
    Site location and shared advertising
    Livery
    Window displays
    Point-of-sale displays
    Fixtures and layout of store
    Lighting

Other types of promotion
    Flyers
    Posters
    Handouts
    Hot air balloons
    Sandwich boards

Choosing the right promotional mix for your business calls for professional skills. Check with your advertising and/or public relations agency.

Figure 7.4   *Promotion = Time + Money*

Time must be set aside for:

Task	Persons involved	Frequency
Long- and short-term market planning	Key staff	Annually
Strategic planning for promotions	Key staff Agency	Semi-annually
Discussion of marketing and promotional objectives	All staff	Quarterly
Discussion and evaluation of specific promotional activities and materials	All staff	Before and after each campaign
Implementation and scheduling	You Ad agency	Monthly or as necessary

Other important time-intensive promotional efforts include development and production of materials, all public relations activities, development and purchase of mailing lists, coordination of bulk mailings, writing and mailing individual letters and proposals, telephone, mail, and personal follow-up of promotional efforts.

Money must be set aside for:

Public relations and general information materials
    Printing
    Photograhy
    Sponsorship of events
    Open days, factory visits
    Mailings
    Donations
    Memberships (Rotary, Chamber of Commerce, etc)

Targeted product and service campaigns
Copywriting and design fees
Media placement costs
Photography, typesetting and graphic-design costs
Printing
Bulk mail (fulfilment)
Mailing lists
Studio and talent costs of radio/TV spot production
Advertising agency fees other than for copy and design

Reducing advertising costs when business starts to slow down will only accelerate a sales slump, not save your profitability.

Incomplete campaigns just eat up money – see Figure 7.4. You might as well burn the cash and save the time; you'd come out ahead.

Question 24: What is your advertising and promotion budget? If you don't have an advertising and promotion budget, you don't have a rational marketing plan.

Advertising and promotion are a cost of doing business. Rigorously and ruthlessly suppress the urge to cut it at the first sign of sluggish sales. Build it in, like payments on plant or equipment or any other fixed cost, and be prepared to increase it. An advertising campaign is like a military campaign. Attaining your objectives calls for careful allocation and concentration of your resources so that you can successfully implement your strategy.

You buy and maintain market share with advertising as well as with product, service, distribution and other business efforts. When sales are off, increase advertising efforts. When sales are up, you may be able to ease off a little – run ads less often, for example. Reducing advertising costs when business starts to slow down will only accelerate a sales slump, not save your profitability.

How do you set an advertising budget? There are four common methods:

1. *Percentage of sales.* You can get trade figures to show how others in your industry allocate their advertising budget. Base this on your anticipated or desired sales, and treat advertising and promotion as a fixed expense. If sales levels or goals increase, change the advertising budget. Do not cut advertising budgets in response to short-term sales slumps.

This method is inflexible, and doesn't reflect the cost structures and marketing goals of your business. It does provide a good baseline. If you differ seriously from industry standards, have a good reason for that variance and be prepared to justify that variance to your bank.

2. *Left-over budget.* This is sometimes arrived at by adding all the other expenses and then allocating what's left to advertising. Another way is to take last year's advertising expenses and increase them by a set percentage or amount.

This leaves your advertising unbudgeted, your campaigns incomplete, and your marketing efforts gutted. Left-over budgeting is far and away the most popular method for small business owners, which offers scope when there is a competitive opening for you to take advantage of.

3. *Project-by-project or ad hoc budgeting.* While this approach may enrich your advertising agency, it is effectively no budget at all. It lets you reduce advertising without noticing that you are doing so. It does have great flexibility, which is a strength if used in conjunction with a budget for continuous advertising and promotional efforts.

4. *Flexible budgeting.* Set a lower limit, based on experience, industry standards, and sales goals. Then be prepared to increase it, on a project basis, to take advantage of opportunities or to turn a sales slump around.

If you insist on doing your own publicity, promotion and advertising, ask yourself once more: What business am I in?

Small business owners who are on the ball use two budgets to support their promotional campaigns. The first is a percentage

105

of sales or left-over budget for current advertising and promotional expenses, while the other is a discretionary budget (project budget) with well-defined applications and cash limits.

Question 25: What are your advertising and promotion objectives?

If you reach your advertising objectives, you should be closer to attaining your marketing objectives. Advertising is tactical rather than strategic – see Figure 8.3, Strategies and tactics, on page 123 for a more detailed explanation. Your advertising goals serve your marketing goals, not vice versa.

Figure 7.5 Advertising/Promotion goals

These are goals some astute small business owners have set for their advertising and promotional campaigns. They are intended to nudge your thinking, not as a comprehensive list of goals.

Do you want to:

1. Penetrate specialised markets? Which ones? What are the measures of progress (unit sales, cash turnover, other benchmarks)?
2. Sell more to present customers? How?
3. Specialise in terms of product or services? Which ones? Why?
4. Change your business's image? Why? To what? How?
5. Penetrate geographical markets more deeply? Which areas? How?
6. Create 'top-of-mind' awareness? How?
7. Expand demographically? To whom? What market segments?
8. Increase sales of specific product or services? How?
9. Announce a new product/service, new product/service mix, or new location?
10. Support community projects for public relations benefits?

Use the answers to these questions to help decide how you want to be perceived, who you plan to do business with, and what you want to sell.

Question 26: How do you promote your business?

If you insist on doing your own publicity, promotion and advertising, ask yourself once more, 'What business am I in?' If it isn't self-promotion, then you'd do better to rely on outside advisers to help you set and implement your advertising and promotional policies. This is a specialised field, and too important an area for amateur efforts.

Figure 7.6 *Initial advertising agenda*

When you work with an advertising agent or public relations expert, the first item on their agenda will be to decide:

1. What business are you in?
2. What do you want to accomplish with your advertising, publicity, or promotion?
3. What do you sell?
4. To whom?
5. What are your sales and marketing goals?
6. What's your budget?
7. What's your timetable for achieving your goals?

You can simplify much of the groundwork that effective advertising and promotion require. In fact, most of the work can and should be done by you. After all, it's your vision, experience and intuition that make your business special.

If these seem to be familiar questions, they are. Advertising and promotional campaigns begin with your current situation, rely on the budgetary guidelines to help you reach your goals, and absolutely demand thorough knowledge of what your business is now and will become. And as you've seen by now, these are time-consuming questions to answer. Quick answers just aren't enough. You need facts, documentation, analysis, and more facts. The questions in Figure 7.7 will help to focus your preliminary efforts.

An advertising plan (including promotional efforts) involves eight steps. Now that you know your advertising/promotional budget and your objectives, you can set down a preliminary plan fairly quickly.

1. *Identify long-term objectives.* These are ultimate goals, probably a year or more ahead. As always, make them as precise as you can: turnover or unit sales, time frames, persons responsible for attaining them, some indication of the resources you can allocate to achieving them.

2. *Define short-term goals and priorities.* What do you want to get done next month, next week, tomorrow?

3. *Assemble resources.* Have your in-house information available. A sketch of your options and priorities is helpful. Have your business plan to hand.

4. *Select an advertising agency* to guide you through the thickets of media selection and production scheduling. See Figure 7.8.

Ads alone don't sell – but they create awareness and support your other selling efforts

5. *Schedule projects.* This is the heart of your advertising plan, and calls for a large calendar to help establish timelines. (Figure 7.9 gives you an idea of how much time is involved at each stage of production.) For each advertisement or project, ask:

    A. Where will it run?
    B. What is the 'street date' when it will appear?
    C. What size will it be?
    D. How much will it cost to prepare?
    E. What is the media cost?

Important considerations to keep in mind throughout the plan are timing, repetition (you get bored with the ad before your prospects and customers are aware that it's running), and reinforcement. Ads alone don't sell – but they create awareness and support your other selling efforts. You must spell out deadlines and assign responsibility to one individual (perhaps yourself) to make the most of your budget.

6. *Choose media*. See Figure 7.10.

7. *Specifications for ads.* Usually you leave this to your agency, but if you do it yourself, be sure to include:

A. Purpose of the ad. What do you want to accomplish?
B. Preferred approach. Hard sell? Soft sell? Humour? Fit the approach to your image.
C. Size and frequency of ad.
D. A creative budget.
E. Deadlines.

8. *Evaluate the results.* Unevaluated advertising might give you some short-run advantages, but if you can learn from your advertising and promotional experiences, your advertising can become more effective.

You can test many elements of your advertising by following traditional methods. These work; they have been well proved.

A. Offer coupons.
B. Offer sales of certain items.
C. Split runs of your ad. (For example, run your ad in a national magazine only to certain geographic areas.)
D. Track enquiries. (For example, ask people to 'write to Department XYZ' for more information.)
E. Look for patterns of response (timing, number, percentages).
F. Keep a scrapbook of your ads and other efforts. Keep one for your competitors, too.
G. Check with your staff.
H. Ask customers what they read and watch. See Figure 7.11, Ten-second media quiz.

Summary of Chapter 7

1. You completed a promotion audit (Figure 7.1) to establish where you need professional advertising help.
2. You looked at different ways of promoting your business (Figure 7.3) and what goes into planning a promotional campaign (Figure 7.4). Then you need to set goals and an advertising budget.
3. Figure 7.8 will help you evaluate advertising agencies and choose the one most likely to help you reach your advertising and promotion goals. Figures 7.6 and 7.7 will help you set an agenda with your advertising agency.
4. Work with your agency to develop an advertising action plan. Set a timetable for the objectives you want to reach, when actions will be taken to implement these objectives and how much money will be needed at specific times to achieve your objectives.

Figure 7.7   *Advertising/Promotional questions*

Ask and answer these questions:

1. Markets
   What is your market mix?
   What percentage of your business comes from:
Individuals?	**15%**
Small businesses?	**75%**
Big businesses?	**10%**
Local trade?	**80%**
Regional trade?	**20%**
   National or international trade?
   What is the market potential?

2. Products/Services
   Are they:
   Innovative? ✔
   Specialised?
   Diversified? ✔ *maybe too diversified – a problem*
   Commodity?

Packaged?
Tailor-made or customised? ✓
(Answer 'how' to each 'Yes' answer.)

3. Image
   Would you describe your business as:
      Formal?
      Informal? ✓
      With a community focus?
      With a regional or national focus? } *we can't decide*
      Aggressive?
      Relaxed or laid-back? } *50/50*
      Sophisticated?
      Domestic?
      Specialised?
      General in outlook?
      Does this description fit the way you want to be perceived as well
      as the way you see yourself now? Or do you want to change your
      company's image? *we need to create one*

4. Business strengths
   What special expertise or experience do you have?
   Does your business offer:
      Long establishment in the community?
      Convenient location?
      Outstanding service reputation? ✓
      Other benefits? (specify)

5. Competition
   How do you compare with your competition's:
      Market share? *low penetration*
      Image?

6. Customer base
   Do you sell:
      Many products and services to a few loyal customers? ✓
      Several products to a narrowly defined industry?
      Single products to a diverse client base? ✓

   Do you have a data base to tell you:
      The product mix for each customer? ✓

Where their business came from (referral, advertising, etc)? ✓
The basic demographics of your markets? *we should get one*

Figure 7.8 *Selecting a promotional pro*

When shopping for an advertising or public relations agency, ask:

1. *What process does your agency use in analysing client needs?*
A successful programme includes as much or more planning as execution. You want to be sure that the agency has the 'mental horsepower' to see beyond the obvious and move your promotional programmes beyond the limits of your own abilities.

2. *Once you've ascertained my needs, how will you position my company?*
The agency has to be your partner in developing a creative strategy for your business. What process do they use to develop your communications goals? Why?

3. *How do you measure the effectiveness of your strategies?*
Results can be measured in attitude changes, exposure, awareness, sales increases, specific information requested – and other ways. Make sure you are comfortable with their measurement plans, and that you understand why those are valid measurements. Be very wary of 'You can't measure the results, but . . .' excuses. If it can't be measured, you can't afford it.

4. *How do you keep us informed about your activities?*
You should get tear sheets, comprehensive and understandable billing, and full explanations of what is going on when you request it.

5. *Who else have you worked with, especially firms like mine? What success (and horror) stories do you have? Whom may we contact?*
Customers, both happy and unhappy, provide the least biased information about how well performance matched expectations.

6. *Describe a successful programme for a business like ours. What were the goals of the programme? What strategies and tactics did you use? How did you measure your success?*
You want to separate fact from selling. Ask for names and numbers.

7. *If the campaign is public relations (unpaid advertising), what are your relation-ships with the media? Are you on a first-name basis with 'influencers' in our field?*
Nothing is as helpful as a personal friend in high places. PR firms work to establish these relationships, and are (usually) proud of them.

8. *How do you approach creativity? How do you measure it? How do you involve clients in the creative process?*
The aim is to find out if they value creativity as a tool (good) or as an end in itself (bad). This is a judgement call you have to make.

9. *What important clients have you lost in the past year? Why did you lose them? May I speak to them?*
An agency that runs down a former client will eventually criticise you. Every agency loses clients to their competition; good agents know why and aren't ashamed or antagonistic about it.

10. *Most important of all, who will be working on our account day by day?*
You want to have experienced talent working for you, not the newest recruit. You can't afford to train beginners. Make sure the agency's top talent is working for you.

Figure 7.9 *Production timelines*

	Print ad	Two-colour brochure	Coupon	Letter/ Press release
Choose publication	1–7 days	Not Applicable	Not Applicable	1–3 days
Assign tasks/ hire professionals	1–2 days	1–2 days	1–2 days	1 day
Write	1–4 days	1–7 days	1–2 days	1–3 days
Edit	1–2 days	1–3 days	1 day	1–2 days
Design	1–4 days	1–7 days	1–2 days	1–2 days*
Get estimates for printing/ choose printer	Not Applicable	1–3 days	1–2 days	1 day
Photography	2–7 days*	2–7 days*	Not Applicable	2–7 days*
Illustration	2–7 days*	2–7 days*	Not Applicable	Not Applicable
Paste-up	2–4 days	2–7 days	1–2 days	1–2 days*
Printing/ proofing	Not Applicable	1–3 weeks	1–3 days	1–3 days
Total time	1–4 weeks	2–6 weeks	1–2 weeks	1–2 weeks

*If necessary

Figure 7.10 *Media advantages and disadvantages at a glance*

	Advantages	Disadvantages
Newspapers	• Your ad has size and shape, and can be as large as necessary to communicate as much of a story as you care to tell. • The distribution of your message can be limited to your geographic area. • Split-run tests are available to test your copy and your offer. • Free help is usually available to create and produce your ad. • Speed. The ad you decide to run today can be in your customer's hands two days from now.	• Clutter – your ad has to compete for attention with large ads run by supermarkets and department stores. • Poor photo reproduction limits creativity. • A price-oriented medium – most ads are for sales. • Short shelf life. The day after a newspaper appears, it's history. • Waste circulation. You're paying to send your message to a lot of people who will probably never be in the market to buy from you • A highly visible medium. Your competitors can quickly react to your prices.
Magazines	• High reader involvement means more attention will be paid to your advertisement. • Less waste circulation. You can place your ads in magazines read primarily by buyers of your product or service. • Better quality paper permits better photo reproduction and full colour ads. • The smaller page (generally 8½ × 11 inches) permits even small ads to stand out.	• Long lead times (generally 90 days) means you have to make plans a long time in advance. • Higher space costs plus higher creative costs.
Yellow Pages	• Everyone uses the Yellow Pages. • Ads are reasonably inexpensive. • You can easily track responses.	• All your competitors are listed, so you run the ad as a defensive measure. • Ads are not very creative, since they follow certain formats.

	Advantages	Disadvantages
Radio	• A universal medium – enjoyed at home, at work, and while driving. Most people listen to the radio at one time or another during the day. • Permits you to target your advertising spend to the market most likely to respond to your offer. • Permits you to create a personality for your business using only sounds and voices. • Free creative help is usually available. • Rates can generally be negotiated. • Least inflated medium. During the past ten years, radio rates have gone up less than other media.	• Listeners cannot refer back to your ads to go over important points. • Ads are an interruption to the entertainment. Because of this, radio ads must be repeated to break through the listener's 'tune-out' factor. • Radio is a background medium. Most listeners are doing something else while listening, which means your ad has to work hard to be listened to and understood. • Advertising costs are based on ratings which are approximations based on diaries kept in a relatively small fraction of a region's homes.
Television	• Permits you to reach great numbers of people on a national or regional level. • Independent stations and cable offer new opportunities to pinpoint local audiences. • Very much an image-building medium.	• Creative and production costs can quickly mount up. • Preferred slots are often sold out far in advance. • Most ads are 10 or 30 seconds long, which limits the amount of information you can communicate.
Direct mail	• Your advertising message is targeted to those most likely to buy your product or service. • Your message can be as long as necessary to tell your story fully. • You have total control over all elements of creation and production.	• Long lead times required for creative printing and mailing. • Requires coordinating the services of many people: artists, photographers, printers, etc. • People move, so you must work hard to keep your mailing list up to date.

	Advantages	Disadvantages
	• A 'silent' medium. Your message is hidden from your competitors until it's too late for them to react.	• Likewise, a certain percentage of the names on a purchased mailing list is likely to be no longer useful.
Telemarketing	• You can easily answer questions about your product/service. • It's easy to prospect and find the right person to talk to. • Cost effective compared with direct sales. • Highly measurable results. • You can get a lot of information if your script is properly structured.	• Lots of businesses use tele-marketing. • Professionals should draft the script and perform the tele-marketing in order for it to be effective. • Can be extremely expensive. • Most appropriate for high-price retail items or professional services.
Speciality Advertising (balloons, sand-wich boards, key rings, etc)	• Can be attention grabbers if they are done well. • Can give top-of-mind awareness. • Gets your name in front of people.	• Difficult to target your market. • Can be an inappropriate medium for some businesses. • It's difficult to find items that are appropriate for certain businesses.

Figure 7.11 *Ten-second media quiz*   This really doesn't apply to us.

Please list the newspapers you read regularly.

	Daily	Weekly
1. First choice	_____	_____
2. Second choice	_____	_____
3. Third choice	_____	_____

Please list the radio stations you listen to regularly.

1. First choice   _____
2. Second choice   _____
3. Third choice   _____
4. Fourth choice   _____
5. Fifth choice   _____

Have you recently seen or heard our advertising?

Where?   _____

Thank you for your help!

Your logo

◀ CHAPTER 8 ▶

STRATEGIC MARKETING

All marketing decisions are strategic. Strategic marketing takes account of the competitive nature of business and keeps your efforts focused. All the preceding chapters have implicitly taken a strategic bent; now you want to make your own strategy explicit.

Why consciously choose a marketing strategy? Your marketing efforts are goal-directed, and you want to be sure that the goals you are aiming at are the goals you wish to reach. Strategic planning makes sure that you do the right things. Your marketing plan helps you do those things right.

Question 27: What marketing problems have you discovered so far?
All businesses have problems. The strengths of your competition, your business's competitive weakness, technological changes, shifting public tastes – the list can go on and on.

Look again at Figures 1.6, 2.2, 2.5, 4.3, 4.4, 4.5, and all of Chapter 6, especially Figure 6.3.

Ask yourself (and your staff and other interested persons):

Strategic planning makes sure that you do the right things. Your marketing plan helps you do those things right.

1. What marketing problems are we currently working on?
2. What problems are we avoiding?
3. What are we going to do about them?
4. Who is responsible for solving these problems – and when? With what resources?
5. Why haven't we reached our sales and/or marketing goals in the past?
6. What might keep us from reaching our current sales goals?

Question 28: How do you plan to solve these problems?
List several possible solutions to each major problem. Don't just pick the first solution that occurs to you. It probably isn't the best one. The trick is to define the problem as factually as possible, then look for a number of possible causes. Facts and analysis will prevent you from finding a remedy for the symptom rather than the disease.

Then ask yourself how your strategies will affect or be affected by these problems.

If problems have to be resolved, assign responsibility for solving each problem to one person. Make sure to allow enough authority and sufficient resources to that person (you or someone else). Perhaps the solution will involve brainstorming or other techniques. The important thing is first to recognise the problem, then carefully define and analyse it before taking action.

Question 29: Are the goals stated in Chapter 1 still valid? If not, what are your new goals?
Return to Figures 1.3 and 1.5.

Preliminary goal-setting is a starting point, not your final decision. Revise your sales and marketing goals in the light of the analysis in the preceding chapters. Perhaps the strategies that make the best sense for your business call for a revision of your goals.

Figure 8.1 *Problem-solving worksheet*

By: _GL_   Date: _24/2/89_

1. What is the problem? Cite standard and variance from standard if available.

   We lack a single focus

2. Possible causes:

   We've always taken all business which comes our way, and not established a niche for ourselves

3. Interim solution:
   ① Define short-term market goal: Go after car market.
   ② Do a profitability study to determine where time gets billed and where time is wasted.

If you do change some of your goals, what are the new ones? Collect them on Figure 8.2. Be as specific as you can, for example:

For next year:
1. Increase sales of Product A 15 per cent by December;
2. Reduce reject rate by 5 per cent in the next quarter;
3. Open branch office in Manchester in six months, with sales goals and budgets established by Herbert and approved by Maude due on my desk no later than 15 September.

And so forth. Goals have to be clear, measurable, and most important of all, easy to communicate. Your marketing strategies and plan are built to accomplish these goals – and people have to know what the goals are. Fuzzy goals such as 'Increase sales' or 'Cut the reject rate' or 'Get that dratted branch going' are seriously deficient, don't provide the timetables or assign responsibilities, and as a result are not effective.

Figure 8.2 *Personal and business goal summary*

Personal goals include non-financial goals as well as financial goals. Limit the goals to the most important.

1. List your personal goals.
   A. Improve health and increase level of energy
   B. Change the mix of work I'm currently doing
   C. Make more time to enjoy life
   D. Make more money
   E.

2. List your business goals.

	For next year:	In three years:
Quantitative goals:		
A. Sales (£)	£175,000	£265,000
B. Sales (unit)		
C. Profit (£)	£50,000	£100,000
D. Profit (% sales)		(at least!)
E. Market share		
F. Company net worth (£)		
G. Number of employees	5	8

Qualitative goals:
   A. Market position small-business experts   more niche oriented
   B. Kind of business accounting   more business
   C. Target markets   car business   consulting Co's   consulting
   D. Business culture or style Same   even more professional
   E. Other (specify)
       Improve use of time

3. Potential conflicts between personal and business goals. We need to work out a marketing plan so all business goals reflect our personal goals. Need more personnel if we are to grow.
4. Comments

Question 30: How do you plan to achieve these goals?
That's what your marketing plan is all about. Each goal calls for a series of actions. The strategies in Figure 8.4 set broad marketing objectives; the more specific goals in Figure 8.2 define the tactical boundaries. You won't attain your goals all at once, but rather in stages.

If you have chosen your strategies wisely, and made sure that reaching the goals of Figure 8.2 lead to attaining the strategic objectives, the steps should be clear. As with any other tactical plan, you have to know what the goal is, when it is to be reached, what you have by way of resources to attain that goal, and what the possible barriers are. Some of these details will be spelled out in Chapter 10, The Sales Plan. Others will be treated in the marketing plan itself.

Figure 8.3 *Strategies and tactics*

All strategic elements must be defined in terms of needs, attitudes, and unmet desires in the market. These will include known needs that can be accurately pinpointed by investigation and hypothetical needs that must be nourished to become a market need.

Tactics are:	Strategies are:
Concrete	Conceptual
Specific	General
Individual	Complex
Linear	Organic
Sequential	Interactive and systematic

Strategic planning must define qualitative goals. These qualitative goals include:

☐ *Positioning.* What is the position of your organisation in its target markets and among your competitors? How is it viewed by the market?
☐ *Segmentation.* What are the demographics, attitudes, and tastes of your defined target markets?
☐ *Cultural.* What is the culture of your business?

123

□ *Stylistic.* What is the style of your business?
□ *Differentiation.* In what ways does your business and its product/service structure differ from all other organisations offering similar products/services?
□ *Functional.* What purpose does the organisation and its product/service structure fulfil beyond its own parochial needs?

Quantitative elements to be defined include: price, strategy, market share, growth rate, cost characteristics, sales and profit goals, production and distribution goals, and logistics.

Your strategies should reflect your attitudes and personality.

Selecting a marketing strategy is a four-step process:

1. *Examine past and current marketing strategies.* Have yours been 'business as usual', 'get whatever business we can', or 'follow-the-leader'? These are the three most common and least effective strategies for small business owners. Few small business owners plan to run their businesses these ways, but inattention and habit make such choices inevitable.

You can't change strategies overnight. They are built into the culture of your business. Your goals and methods of achieving those goals (including business practices and relationships of people within the business) are inextricably mixed up with your strategic choices. The strategies and culture evolve together slowly; they change slowly, too.

Your strategies should reflect your attitudes and personality. Strategies can be active or reactive, aggressive or defensive, risk-inclined or risk-averse. If your own style is relaxed and risk-averse, an aggressive, high-risk strategy probably won't work. If you enjoy risk and being ahead of the crowd, then a defensive, reactive strategy will drive you up the wall. That doesn't mean that you can't adopt a conflicting strategy for a short while – but if you adopt one counter to your feelings, be aware of the potential conflict.

In Figure 8.4, Checklist for strategic planning, tick off the strategies that best fit your business's past and present practices. While the list is not exhaustive, it encompasses most strategies that small business owners can realistically apply. Don't try to pick the best strategies for your business yet. You have a few steps still to take.

2. *Summarise personal and business objectives.* Include your personal goals in your marketing plans. If you want to retire in five years, fine. Plan for it. If you want to work until you drop, fine. Plan for it. If you want your business to remain small enough so you can bring your dog to work, great. It can be done. Just don't set up your business to thwart yourself. If you want to see how big a business you can build, go ahead. But don't do it unless it makes sense to you personally.

In Figure 1.3 you set down preliminary personal goals. Revise them now. In Figure 1.5, you listed preliminary business goals. Revise them also. If your personal priorities aren't in line with your business priorities, change your business priorities. You have better things to do with your life than warp it for the benefit of your business. Review Figure 8.2. Figure 8.5 should include all changes and revisions of your goals to date; it will be the basis of your marketing plan.

3. *Now return to Figure 8.4.* Examine each of these strategies and ask yourself if, given your resources and competitive situation, each would help you to reach your goals. You will probably want to use more than one strategy, or modify one or more better to fit your business.

4. *Choose the simplest strategies for your business.* To be effective, strategies have to be communicated. Fancy strategies look great on paper, but if they present opportunities for misunderstanding, you can count on their being misunderstood. The simplest strategies are the best strategies.

Now make your final strategic choices.

- ☐ *Test them for consistency with each other.* You don't want to pursue contradictory strategies.
- ☐ *Test them for feasibility.* If they require more resources than you can muster, they won't work.
- ☐ *Test them for coherence.* Do they fit your business? Do they tend to unify the focus of your marketing efforts? Do they form an understandable, easily communicated grand strategy?
- ☐ Finally, *make sure that they are acceptable to your employees.* If you can't generate company-wide support, the strategy will fail. This is where complicated strategies break down. If you can't communicate the strategies clearly, you have a problem. (This is a blessing in disguise. In competitive markets, your competition will look at your strategy and try to improve on it by making it a bit fancier here, a bit more complicated there. Let them be complex. You stay simple, and win the market-place.)

Summary of Chapter 8

1. Marketing problems (and problems that might affect your marketing plans) were listed and addressed in Figure 8.1.
2. Personal and business goals appear twice. Figure 8.2 is based on the earlier goals and objectives, as well as preliminary strategic thoughts. Figure 8.5 is the final result of Chapters 1 to 8.
3. Strategies for your marketing plan are indicated on Figure 8.4; the goals they are to help you attain are listed on Figure 8.5.

Figure 8.4 *Checklist for strategic planning*

This checklist presents a range of small business strategic options proved in hundreds of applications.

Past	Current	Future	Strategy	Probable consequences, risks
			Sample marketing strategies	
1.			Rationalise distribution. Cut back to most efficient network; look at volume, geography, type.	Increase profit margins, reduce stocks, some costs go down; may need new investment; moderate risk.
2.			Develop the market. Create demand for a brand new product.	Very high marketing costs, may increase debtors, impacts profit and loss statement, hinders cash flow; large expense budget; high risks – but high reward if successful.
3.			Penetrate the market. Increase market share: lower price, broaden product line mix, add service and sales personnel, increase advertising.	Increases marketing and sales expenses, need for working capital, and need for capital investment if capacity grows. Reduces short-term earnings; high risk.
4.			Promote new products to present market. Develop, broaden or replace products in product line, sell to present market.	Lower unit costs; increase stock, sales volume, profit and cash flow; some capital investment needed, increased development, design and manufacturing costs; moderate to high risk.

	Past	Current	Future	Strategy	Probable consequences, risks
5.				Seek new markets, same products. Expand existing markets by geography (abroad) or type for existing products.	Increase sales volume and profit margins as unit costs drop and as new market grows; higher short-term selling costs; modest capital investment, increased working capital; high risk.
6.				Develop new products for new markets. Invest in developing, manufacturing and marketing products unrelated to product line for new markets.	Will increase sales volume, costs, profits (if successful); will have some problems as a new business if products unrelated to current line; will need more working capital, may need new capital investment; increase in sales and marketing costs; high risk.
7.				Rationalise market. Prune back to most profitable segments, higher volume segments; concentrate marketing focus.	Reduce sales volume, increase profit margins, reduce working capital needs, increase cash flow as percentage of sales, decrease debtors; willingness to accept lower sales totals; moderate risk.
8.				Maintain products and market share. Business continues as before; same products, same markets.	Increase at industry growth rate with stable, short-term profit margins; decrease working capital and increase cash inflow over time; may reduce unit costs; investment in strategies to hold position; low risk.

Past	Current	Future	Strategy	Probable consequences, risks
			Sample management strategies	
9.			Cut costs. Reduce costs uniformly through management edicts.	Increase profit margins, achieve lowest possible returns of all efficiency strategies; needs excellent implementation to apply intelligently; moderate risks due to arbitrary nature of cutbacks – may have invidious consequences.
10.			Abandon unit. Sell or liquidate unit because it doesn't fit in with company – or because it is worth more to someone else.	Improve cash flow from sale of assets, create possible morale problem in rest of organisation; low risk.
			Sample financial strategies	
11.			Rationalise product line. Narrow profit line to most profitable items.	Reduce sales volume, improve working capital, profitability, may lead to underusing assets in short term; hard to give up old winners; low to moderate risk.
12.			Pure survival. Cut down to meet most adverse conditions by eliminating or paring down some aspects of the business.	Reduce sales volume, considerably reduce costs, improve ROI short term, improve cash flow temporarily; courage needed, moderate risk due to possible loss of market share, some danger from creditors and other trade sources.

Past	Current	Future	Strategy	Probable consequences, risks
13.			Pause in action. Slow down or establish a one-year moratorium on new capital investment; normal maintenance of business.	No effect on sales short term, may disrupt growth plans, weaken business over long term, decrease sales and earnings if pause is too lengthy; courage and large measure of steadfastness; low risk.
			Sample production strategies	
14.			Improve technology. Improve operating efficiency through techno-logical improvements in physical plant, equipment, or processes.	Decrease variable costs and increase fixed costs – an overall reduction can considerably increase profits, affects sales volume slightly; low to high capital investment; low to moderate risk depending on the extent to which the particular technology is proven.
			Sample operating strategies	
15.			Improve methods and functions. Invest in new ways of doing existing tasks by adding new 'soft' technologies; eg, new patterns of work flow, CAD/CAM, production planning and inventory control, etc, to improve effectiveness and/or efficiency.	Improve operating performance, improve functional rather than product costs; expense investment; creative thinking needed; low to moderate risk.

Figure 8.5 *Personal and business goal summary*

1. List your personal goals.
   A.
   B.
   C.
   D.
   E.

Let's think about this some more and review it next week!

2. List your business goals.

	For next year:	In three years:

Quantitative goals:
   A. Sales (£)
   B. Sales (unit)
   C. Profit (£)
   D. Profit (% sales)
   E. Market share
   F. Company net worth (£)
   G. Number of employees

Qualitative goals:
   A. Market position
   B. Kind of business
   C. Target markets
   D. Business culture or style
   E. Other (specify):

   _____

   _____

3. Potential conflicts between personal and business goals:

4. Comments:

◀ CHAPTER 9 ▶

THE MARKETING PLAN

Your overriding marketing objective is to find people to buy enough of your products and services, for enough money and often enough, to ensure a solid profit margin.

Now you can assemble your marketing plan.

Your overriding marketing objective is to find people to buy enough of your products and services, for enough money and often enough, to ensure a solid profit margin. Your marketing plan helps keep your business focused on the steps necessary to reach or exceed your goals.

Your marketing plan should not be long. If it becomes much longer than 20 pages, it won't be used. Individual elements that back it up may be lengthy, however. An advertising/promotional plan, for example, may run much longer. Sales plans for individual products, product lines, or services can become immensely detailed (see Chapter 10).

The marketing plan must be succinct. It summarises the analyses and strategies of the preceding eight chapters – so in one sense, you've already written it. Writing out your formal marketing plan gives you another chance to review your ideas and goals. If you haven't involved your staff in the planning process, this is a good time to get their ideas.

The key section of your marketing plan (Figure 9.2) is Section 7:

How will you attain your goals? You have four strategic variables to play with: Product/Service, Price, Location, and Promotion. Each can be subdivided further (see Figure 9.1) and tailored to meet the wants of your target markets.

There is no mechanical method to work out how to reach your goals. Your judgement and experience have to find expression here. The most common reason strategies fail is that the fundamentals of implementing the game plan are done poorly or not at all. It doesn't matter how good your strategy is if it isn't properly executed.

The strategic variables must be considered in the light of your present and prospective target markets. In fact, all your marketing plans should focus on meeting the needs and wants of these markets.

Figure 9.1 *Aspects of the four strategic marketing variables*

Make sure the aspects of each variable that pertain to your business complement one another.

Product/Service
  New, modified, new application
  Position on life cycle
    Cash cow?
    Rising star?
    Dog?
    Owner's ego?
  Benefits to purchaser
  Perceived value

Price
  To end user
  To distributors and to trade
    (What margins do you allow distributors and trade?)
  Image
  Market penetration
  Market's sensitivity to price changes

Place
Location
Signs
Direct mail
Direct sales
Telemarketing

Promotion
Advertising (including Yellow Pages, classified ads, and so on)
Public relations
Trade shows
Packaging
Special promotions (sales, spotlights, etc)
Personal selling
Sales force training
Marketing support
Image: point of sale, layout, lighting, stocking
Personal letters

Figure 9.2 *Suggested outline of marketing plan*

1. **Mission statement**
   (What you want your business, main markets and products/services to be.)
2. **Marketing objectives for next year and for the next three years**
   (These are the broad marketing objectives of Figure 1.5.)
3. **Sales and profit goals for the next year and the next three years**
   (See Figure 1.5.)
4. **Products/Services**
   (Brief description by product/service lines, including proposed changes and any recent changes that would affect marketing goals. See Figure 2.3.)
5. **Target markets**
   (List and briefly describe. See Figure 2.4.)
6. **Market potential**
   (What size are the markets and what potential sales, profit, or other advantages does each have? See Figure 3.6.)
7. **How will you attain your goals?**
   A. Overall strategy (See Figure 8.4.)
   B. Competitive strategies (See Figure 4.6.)

C. Promotion strategies (See Figure 7.3.)
D. Pricing, location and sales practices (Brief statement of pricing strategy from Figure 5.3, plus brief statements about location, hours and selling practices from Chapter 5 if important or changed from normal patterns.)
E. Marketing and advertising budgets
8. **Potential problems**
(Brief description, plus proposed solutions, from Figure 8.1.)
9. **Implemention and measurement of timetables and benchmarks**
(See Figure 10.2, Sales and marketing timetables.)
10. **Review and evaluation schedule**
(Short schedule of important review dates.)

Appendix. Include supporting documents such as letters of intent, purchase agreements and so forth if you think documentation is needed.

◄ CHAPTER 10 ►

THE SALES PLAN

The marketing plan defines the strategic directions for your business's marketing. The sales plan is the implementation tool for those grand strategies. Use Figure 10.1, Marketing action plan, and Figure 10.2, Marketing action timetable to help organise actions and assign responsibility for their achievement. The goals come from your marketing plan (see Figures 8.2 and 8.5). The strategic boundaries (permissible methods, resources available, competitive considerations and so on) are your responsibility – and must be considered in setting down the action steps.

Three major guidelines to keep in mind here are:

1. Establishing objective and measurable goals with deadlines. Broad, vaguely defined sales goals are useless.
2. Assigning one person (yourself, perhaps) to oversee the action steps. Shared responsibility means nobody is responsible.
3. Discussing the action steps, timetables, and resources with the person responsible for attaining the objectives. If possible, involve everyone who works on the objective; this helps to ensure their cooperation. If your employees know clearly what you are trying to achieve, why it is important

136

to attain that goal in time and within the resources allotted, and how progress will be measured, they will think up ways to reach that goal.

There are six steps to the marketing action plan:

1. State the goal.
2. Assign a target date for achieving the overall objective.
3. Assign responsibility to a single person.
4. Define the action steps. Achieving the objective requires that certain action steps be taken, in a logical sequence. The more definitive the action steps, the better, since they can be more easily monitored.
5. For each action step, assign a target date. You may also want to assign responsibility for finishing the step to another person; delegation may be the only way to attain these goals. Include the resources needed for each action step, and keep track of them. (Budgets are needed here, but that's another matter.)
6. Track the results, for progress and for future use.

The purpose of Figure 10.1 is to help you put together a tactical plan. Achieving the broad marketing objectives is like winning a war, while reaching these goals is like winning individual battles. The tactics – the short-term activities which must be marshalled to reach the strategic objectives – are highly detailed, but governed by the broad strategic guidelines established beforehand. Tactics only make sense in the context of strategy, otherwise they are just random, undirected actions.

You may wish to break this process down even further, and fill in one of these forms for each goal and each major action step involved. For example, if your goal is to increase net profits from Product A by £10,000 by the end of the next quarter, you might find that you have a considerable number of action steps to take: recruiting and training a new salesperson; preparation of marketing support, advertising and promotional materials; repackaging and repositioning the product; opening a new tar-

Tactics only make
sense in the context of
strategy.

Figure 10.1 *Marketing action plan*

By:_____GL_____   Date:___27/2/89____

Strategic objective:

Action steps	Target date	Person responsible	Results
1) Identify 100 prospects	ASAP 3/89	G , B	
2) Call on prospects in reverse order of desirability – 3 each week	9/89	G , B	
3) Make proposals to 10	11/89	G , B	
4) Close 3	12/89	G , B	

get market – all the while making sure that it doesn't affect other lines.

Once you have arrived at the action steps and their tentative due dates, timing becomes more and more important. One way to handle the timing problem is to work backwards from the target dates. When do you have to start an action step? What steps along the way are critical to reaching the target dates? The more of these intermediate dates you can establish the better; they provide benchmarks to help keep the process of attaining the goals (and hence the strategic objectives) on schedule.

Use your judgement in choosing which steps to pin down to the tight scheduling of Figure 10.2. You want to strike a balance between no controls and too much control.

Figure 10.2 *Marketing action timetable*

By:_____GL_____ Date:__28/2/89____

Action step:__Identify prospects__ Target date:__4/89__

Completed: Not completed but due:

                                          7/4/89
List the:

Sub-steps	Completion criterion (benchmark)	Date of completion
1. Yellow Pages	15/3/89	12/3/89
2. D, B	22/3/89	13/3/89
3. Drive around	1/4/89	7/4/89
4. Clip ads from local papers	ongoing	ongoing
5.		
6.		

Summary of Chapter 10

1. Figures 10.1 and 10.2 provide an implementation and control system for your marketing plan.
2. If you assign product line (or service line) responsibility to an employee or colleague, work through these figures with him or her. The more people involved in setting the due dates and completion criteria the better – and their ideas on implementation can make a great contribution.
3. A sales plan is simply a compilation of Figures 10.1 and 10.2 for each product and/or service. Since you work out the detailed steps one by one with the overall marketing plan

strategies in mind, reaching these more limited goals will help you to attain the marketing objectives.

4. The reviews and evaluations help to keep the plan on time and on target – and will help you improve your skills.

5. The marketing plan is a strategic plan, that is, it makes sure that you do the right things. The sales plan is tactical; it helps you to do things right. You need both.

APPENDICES

◀ APPENDIX 1 ▶

SUMMARY OF QUESTIONS AND MARKETING PLAN OUTLINE

Part One: Summary of major questions in this book

Chapter 1. Marketing Overview

Question 1: What business are you in?

Question 2: What do you sell?

Question 3: What are your target markets?

Question 4: What are your marketing goals for next year? Your sales and profit goals?

Question 5: What might keep you from achieving these goals?

Question 6: What is your marketing budget?

Chapter 2. Products and Services

Question 7: What are the benefits provided by your products/services?

Question 8: What is special about your products/services?

Question 9: Which product/service is the best contributor to your overhead and profits? Which product/service is the biggest drain on your overheads and profits?

Chapter 3. Customers and Prospects

Questions 10: Who are your current customers?

Question 11: What are their buying habits?

Question 12: Why do your customers buy your goods/services?

Question 13: Who are your best customers and prospects?

Question 14: What is your market share?

Question 14A: Is your market share growing, shrinking or stable?

Question 14B: Is the market growing, shrinking or stable? Is it changing in other ways?

Chapter 4. Competitive Analysis

Question 15: Who are your competitors?

Question 16: What do your competitors do better than you?

Question 17: What do you do better than your competitors?

Question 18: What is your competitive position?

Chapter 5. Price, Location and Sales Practices

Question 19: How do you establish prices?

Question 20: How does your location affect you?

Question 21: What are your sales practices?

Chapter 6. Strengths and Weaknesses

Question 22: What is your business strong at?

Question 23: What is your business weak at?

Chapter 7. Advertising and Promotion

Question 24: What is your advertising and promotion budget?

Question 25: What are your advertising and promotion objectives?

Question 26: How do you promote your business?

Chapter 8. Strategic Marketing

Question 27: What marketing problems have you discovered so far?

Question 28: How do you plan to solve these problems?

Question 29: Are the goals stated in Chapter 1 still valid? If not, what are your new goals?

Question 30: How do you plan to achieve these goals?

Part Two: Outline of a marketing plan

1. **Mission statement**
   (What you want your business, main markets and products/services to be.)

2. **Marketing objectives for the next year and for the next three years**
   (These are the broad marketing objectives of Figure 1.5.)

3. **Sales and profit goals for the next year and the next three years**
   (See Figure 1.5.)

4. Products/Services
(Brief description by product/service lines, including proposed changes and any recent changes that would affect marketing goals. See Figure 2.3.)

5. Target markets
(List and briefly describe. See Figure 2.4.)

6. Market potential
(What size and potential sales, profit, or other advantages do these have? See Figure 3.6.)

7. How will you attain your goals?
A. Overall strategy (See Figure 8.4.)
B. Competitive strategies (See Figure 4.6.)
C. Promotion strategies (See Figures 7.3. and 7.12.)
D. Pricing, location and sales practices (Brief statement of pricing strategy from Figure 5.3, plus brief statements about location, hours and selling practices from Chapter 5 if important or changed from normal patterns.)
E. Marketing and advertising budgets

8. Potential problems
(Brief description, plus proposed solutions, from Figure 8.1.)

9. Implementation and measurement of timetables and benchmarks
(See Figure 10.2, Sales and marketing timetables.)

10. Review and evaluation schedule
(Short schedule of important review dates)

Appendix. Include supporting documents such as letters of intent, purchase agreements and so forth if you think documentation is needed.

◄ APPENDIX 2 ►

BIBLIOGRAPHY

Many excellent business publications, issued by government departments and professional practices, are free. The Small Firms Service is a useful contact (dial operator on 100 and ask for Freefone Enterprise).

Kogan Page publish an extensive list of books for small and medium-sized businesses, as well as for managers and executives. Those particularly helpful to the reader of this book are likely to be:

The Business Plan Workbook, Colin and Paul Barrow, 1988
Buying for Business, Tony Attwood, 1988
Choosing and Using Professional Advisers, 2nd edition, Paul Chaplin, 1986
Commonsense Direct Marketing, 2nd edition, Drayton Bird, 1989
Controlling Cash Flow, David H Bangs, 1989
Customer Service, Malcolm Peel, 1987
Debt Collection Made Easy, Peter Buckland, 1987
Do Your Own Market Research, Paul N Hague and Peter Jackson, 1987
Effective Advertising: The Daily Telegraph Guide for the Small Business, H C Carter, 1986
Effective Use of Market Research, Robin Birn, 1988

Export for the Small Business, 2nd edition, Henry Deschampsneufs
Financial Management for the Small Business, 2nd edition, Colin Barrow, 1988
Getting Sales, Richard D Smith and Ginger Dick, 1984
How to Make Exhibitions Work for Your Business, John Talbot, 1989
Law for the Small Business, 6th edition, Patricia Clayton, 1988
Making Marketing Work, Gerard Earls and Patrick Forsyth, 1989
Market and Sales Forecasting, Gordon J Bolt, 1987
Marketing Without a Marketing Budget, Craig S Rice, 1989
Sales Promotion, Julian Cummins, 1989
Stoy Hayward Business Tax Guide, annual
Successful Marketing for the Small Business, 2nd edition, Dave Patten, 1989

◀ APPENDIX 3 ▶
EXTRA FORMS

This appendix contains all the worksheets from this book. We have provided two copies of certain worksheets for those of you who sell more than one product/service.

Please feel free to copy these forms for your *personal business use* only. Please note, however, that they are protected under copyright law, and large-scale photocopying or reproduction for commercial purposes or republication is strictly forbidden without the prior permission in writing of Kogan Page Limited, 120 Pentonville Road, London N1 9JN.

Table of Contents

Figure 1.2 *Product/Service and market list*

If you have many products/services, try to bundle them together into no more than 10 categories. You can always expand the list later – but for now, keep it simple.

	Product/Service	Target markets
1.	_____	_____
2.	_____	_____
3.	_____	_____
4.	_____	_____
5.	_____	_____
6.	_____	_____
7.	_____	_____
8.	_____	_____
9.	_____	_____
10.	_____	_____

Figure 1.3 *Your personal goals*

1. How much money do you want, or need, to earn?_____
_____
_____
_____

2. What sort of lifestyle is desirable for you and your family?_____
_____
_____
_____

3. How big do you want your business to be?_____
_____
_____
_____

4. How will your business reflect you and your values?_____
_____
_____
_____

5. What are your risk parameters? What is your tolerance for risk?_____
_____
_____
_____

6. What do you want to achieve in five years?_____
_____
_____
_____

Figure 1.4 *Sales approach*

For each product/service or product line, estimate what sales would be if everything goes wrong next year. Then estimate what sales would be if everything goes perfectly. Since neither case is likely, an in-between sales figure will be a more accurate forecast.

Sales forecast

Product/Service	Worst case	Most likely case	Best case
1.			
2.			
3.			
4.			
5.			
6.			
7.			
8.			
9.			
10.			

Figure 1.5 *Preliminary marketing, sales and profit goals*

Marketing goals

1. _____

2. _____

3. _____

Sales goals for each product/service (see Figure 1.4 for next year's most likely figures)

	For next year	In three years
1. _____	£_____	£_____
2. _____	£_____	£_____
3. _____	£_____	£_____
4. _____	£_____	£_____
5. _____	£_____	£_____
6. _____	£_____	£_____
7. _____	£_____	£_____
8. _____	£_____	£_____
9. _____	£_____	£_____
10. _____	£_____	£_____
Profit goals	£_____	£_____

Comments:_____

_____

_____

_____

_____

Figure 1.6 *Obstacles we could face*

Today's date:_____

What problems am I avoiding?_____

1. _____

2. _____

3. _____

What problems might prevent us from reaching our marketing, sales, and profit goals?

1. _____

2. _____

3. _____

4. _____

5. _____

What are we going to do about these problems?

1. Assign responsibility to individuals to achieve solutions.

2. Allocate resources and authority to these people.

3. Establish benchmarks and deadlines to help them monitor their progress.

Figure 1.7 *Marketing budget items*

This is not an exhaustive list. Use it as a starting point. Your company will use some of these categories plus others peculiar to your marketing needs.

1. Selling (direct costs)

    Sales salaries and commissions   £_____

    Travel   £_____

    Entertainment   £_____

2. Selling (indirect costs)

    Training   £_____

    Marketing research   £_____

    Statistical analysis   £_____

    Subscriptions and dues   £_____

3. Advertising   £_____

4. Sales promotion other than advertising   £_____

5. Public relations   £_____

6. Shipping and handling

    Order filling, packaging   £_____

    Postage and cartage   £_____

7. Credits and collection

    Administrative expense   £_____

    Bad debt allowance   £_____

8. Marketing administration   £_____

9. Other items   £_____

Figure 1.8 *Preliminary marketing budget estimates*

Made by:_____   Date:_____

Reviewed by:_____   Date:_____

Goal or action: (eg, Advertising	Timing: monthly	Costs: £750/month)
_____	_____	_____
_____	_____	_____
_____	_____	_____
_____	_____	_____
_____	_____	_____
_____	_____	_____

Total: £_____

Use this for rough estimates only. You need your accountant's help in setting up your final marketing budget.

Figure 2.2 *Product comparison form*

Fill this in for each product or service you offer. For the sake of simplicity, compare yours only with the leading competitive products or services.

Product/Service: _____

	Yours	The competition's
Target markets:	_____	_____
Benefits offered:		
1.	_____	_____
2.	_____	_____
3.	_____	_____
Quality	_____	_____
Price	_____	_____
Improved versions	_____	_____
Location	_____	_____
Delivery	_____	_____
Follow-up service	_____	_____
Availability	_____	_____
Convenience	_____	_____
Reliability	_____	_____
Service	_____	_____
Guarantees	_____	_____
Other (specify)		
1.	_____	_____
2.	_____	_____
3.	_____	_____

Figure 2.2 *Product comparison form*

Fill this in for each product or service you offer. For the sake of simplicity, compare yours only with the leading competitive products or services.

Product/Service: _____

	Yours	The competition's
Target markets:	_____	_____
Benefits offered:		
1.	_____	_____
2.	_____	_____
3.	_____	_____
Quality	_____	_____
Price	_____	_____
Improved versions	_____	_____
Location	_____	_____
Delivery	_____	_____
Follow-up service	_____	_____
Availability	_____	_____
Convenience	_____	_____
Reliability	_____	_____
Service	_____	_____
Guarantees	_____	_____
Other (specify)		
1.	_____	_____
2.	_____	_____
3.	_____	_____

Figure 2.3 *Product/Service application worksheet*

Product/Service:_____

_____

_____

What are its features?_____

_____

_____

What benefits does it produce?_____

_____

_____

How is it used?_____

_____

_____

_____

How is it purchased (unit, bulk, with other products)? Which other products?_____

_____

_____

_____

_____

What are other possible applications of this product/service?_____

_____

_____

_____

_____

Figure 2.3 *Product/Service application worksheet*

Product/Service:_____

_____

_____

What are its features?_____

_____

_____

What benefits does it produce?_____

_____

_____

How is it used?_____

_____

_____

_____

How is it purchased (unit, bulk, with other products)? Which other products?_____

_____

_____

_____

_____

What are other possible applications of this product/service?_____

_____

_____

_____

_____

_____

Figure 2.4 *Product/Service benefits and markets*

	Your product/service	Benefits it offers (wants/needs fulfilled)	Possible target markets
1.			
2.			
3.			
4.			
5.			
6.			
7.			
8.			
9.			
10.			

Figure 2.4 *Product/Service benefits and markets*

	Your product/service	Benefits it offers (wants/needs fulfilled)	Possible target markets
1.			
2.			
3.			
4.			
5.			
6.			
7.			
8.			
9.			
10.			

Figure 2.5 *Winners and losers*

Products/services with major impact on overheads and profits:

Contributors	Amounts
1. _____	£_____
2. _____	_____
3. _____	_____
4. _____	_____
5. _____	_____

Detractors	Amounts
1. _____	£_____
2. _____	_____
3. _____	_____
4. _____	_____
5. _____	_____

Figure 2.8 *New product/service objectives*

Person responsible:_____ Review date:_____

Product/service idea:_____

_____

_____

Benefits it will offer:_____

_____

_____

Target markets:_____

_____

_____

Timing:_____

Anticipated sales: (£ or unit; by quarter)_____

Anticipated costs:

1. Development _____

2. Advertising _____

3. Impact on other products/services_____

4. Other (specify)_____

Comments:_____

_____

_____

Action taken:_____

_____

_____

By:_____ Date:_____

Figure 2.9 *A summary of your product/service goals*

Product/Service:	Sales goals (for each quarter of next year, in pounds or in units)				
	I	II	III	IV	TOTAL
1. _____					
2. _____					
3. _____					
4. _____					
5. _____					
6. _____					
7. _____					
8. _____					
9. _____					
10. _____					

Figure 3.4 *Market segmentation worksheet*

Fill in one of these forms for each of your products/services.

By:_____ Date:_____

Product/Service:

Describe 'ideal customer' according to the criteria listed in Figures 3.2 and 3.3 (see pages 46 and 48 in the text).

Describe their purchasing patterns.

What makes them 'ideal customers' for this product/service?

Figure 3.4 *Market segmentation worksheet*

Fill in one of these forms for each of your products/services.

By:_____ Date:_____

Product/Service:

Describe 'ideal customer' according to the criteria listed in Figures 3.2 and 3.3 (see pages 46 and 48 in the text).

Describe their purchasing patterns.

What makes them 'ideal customers' for this product/service?

Figure 3.5 *Sample survey questions*

Questions on your customer/prospect survey should elicit information about who your customers/prospects are, their buying habits, their opinion of your product/service and their favoured media. Be sure to make the survey easy to fill in – ask simple questions and provide limited choices for answers. For a more complex survey, get professional help from your advertising agency, small business service and local colleges.

Some generic questions might be:

1. Please tell us about yourself.

    Age: 20-30_____ 30-40_____ 40-50_____ 50-60_____ 60-70_____ Over 70_____

    Gender: M_____ F_____

    Marital status: Single_____ Married_____ Divorced_____ Separated_____ Widowed_____

    Do you have children? Yes_____ No_____

    Do you own your home? Yes_____ No_____

    Income level: under £10,000_____   £10,000 to £15,000_____
                   £15,000 to £20,000_____   £20,000 to £30,000_____   over £30,000_____

Occupation _____

Name/Address (optional)_____

_____

2. Do you currently buy our product/use our service?   Yes_____ No_____

    If so, why do you buy from us? _____

    If not, why do you buy from someone else? _____

    Where do you buy (this product/service)?_____

    How often do you buy (this product/service)?_____

3. Could you tell us what you think about our product/service?

    Quality: Excellent_____ Good_____ Fair_____ Poor_____

    How do we compare with (our competitor's product/service)?_____

    How could we improve our (product/service)?_____

4. Where did you see or hear our advertisement?_____

5. What newspapers and magazines do you read?_____

    What are your favourite TV and radio programmes?_____

Figure 3.6 *Customer/Prospect summary form*

By:_____ Date:_____

Reviewed by:_____ Date:_____

These are our most valuable customers and prospects, ranked from the top.
(Make sure you list the market segments and their criteria.)

Name of customer   Market segment   Criteria (see Figure 3.3 on page 48)

1. _____
2. _____
3. _____
4. _____
5. _____

We should target these prospects:

Name of prospect   Market segment   Criteria (see Figure 3.3 on page 48)

1. _____
2. _____
3. _____
4. _____
5. _____

We should consider these market niches:

1. _____
2. _____
3. _____
4. _____
5. _____

Our customer/prospect objectives for the next year are:

1. _____

2. _____

3. _____

Figure 4.1 *Our competitors*

By:_____ Date:_____

My closest competitors are:

1. _____

2. _____

3. _____

4. _____

5. _____

Other competitors (include potential as well as actual) are:

1. _____

2. _____

3. _____

Figure 4.2 *Competitor information*

Prepared by:_____ Date:_____
Competitor:_____
Product/Service:_____
Location(s):_____

Specific information:
 Years in business:_____
 Number of employees:_____
 Value of sales:_____
 Unit sales:_____
 Market share:_____
 Financial strength:_____
 Profitability:_____

Players (include their age, experience in this business, training or education, strengths and weaknesses, and other pertinent information):
 Chairman/owner:_____
 Outside advisers:_____
 Key employees:_____

The competition's marketing strategy:
 Pricing:_____
 Advertising themes:_____
 Promotion/Public relations efforts:_____

Significant changes (new people, products, etc):_____

How this competitor competes with you:_____

Comments:

Figure 4.2 *Competitor information*

Prepared by:_____ Date:_____

Competitor:_____

Product/Service:_____

Location(s):_____

Specific information:

Years in business:_____

Number of employees:_____

Value of sales:_____

Unit sales:_____

Market share:_____

Financial strength:_____

Profitability:_____

Players (include their age, experience in this business, training or education, strengths and weaknesses, and other pertinent information):

Chairman/owner:_____

Outside advisers:_____

Key employees:_____

The competition's marketing strategy:

Pricing:_____

Advertising themes:_____

Promotion/Public relations efforts:_____

Significant changes (new people, products, etc):_____

How this competitor competes with you:_____

Comments:

Figure 4.3 *Comparing myself with my competitors*

Prepared by:_____ Date:_____

Competitor:_____

	Describe your competitor's:	How do you compare?
Price		
Quality		
Service		
Location		
Advertising		
Other yardsticks		

Figure 4.3 *Comparing myself with my competitors*

Prepared by:_____ Date:_____

Competitor:_____

	Describe your competitor's:	How do you compare?
Price		
Quality		
Service		
Location		
Advertising		
Other yardsticks		

Figure 4.4 *Quick comparison – benefits offered to our customers*

	Competitor offers	We offer
Customer seeks:		
Quality		
Exclusivity		
Lower prices		
Product line		
Product service		
Reliability		
Delivery		
Location		
Information		
Availability		
Credit cards		
Credit line		
Guarantee		
Customer advice		
Accessories		
Knowledgeability		
Polite help		

Figure 4.6 *Competitive objectives*

Prepared by:_____ Date:_____

Reviewed by:_____ Date:_____

We need to improve our competitive position in these areas:

1. _____

2. _____

3. _____

We can build on our competitive strengths in these areas:

1. _____

2. _____

3. _____

We can attack our competition in their weak areas:

1. _____

2. _____

3. _____

Figure 5.3 *Price range guidelines*

By:_____   Date:_____

Product/Service:_____

Price range:£_____ to £_____

1. Price floor:

    (a) Mark-on (gross margin) is _____% of retail price.
    (b) Manufacturer's suggested price is £_____.
    (c) Fixed costs are £_____. Variable costs are £_____ or _____% of sales.
    (d) Break-even is £_____.

2. Special considerations for this product's price are:

    ☐ Service   ☐ Overhead
    ☐ Status   ☐ Downtime
    ☐ Quality   ☐ Competition
    ☐ Loss leader   ☐ Market penetration costs
    ☐ Demand   ☐ Other (specify):
    ☐ Product life

3. Turnover rate is _____ times per year.

4. Industry turn average is _____ times per year.

5. Going rate is _____ .

6. I estimate _____ units will be sold.

7. _____ (number of units) at £_____ will cover my fixed costs.

8. Top price possible is £_____. (This estimate is based on the customer's perception of value.)

Comments:

Figure 5.3 *Price range guidelines*

By:_____ Date:_____

Product/Service:_____

Price range:£_____ to £_____

1. Price floor:

    (a) Mark-on (gross margin) is _____% of retail price.
    (b) Manufacturer's suggested price is £_____.
    (c) Fixed costs are £_____. Variable costs are £_____ or _____% of sales.
    (d) Break-even is £_____.

2. Special considerations for this product's price are:

    □ Service   □ Overhead
    □ Status   □ Downtime
    □ Quality   □ Competition
    □ Loss leader   □ Market penetration costs
    □ Demand   □ Other (specify):
    □ Product life

3. Turnover rate is _____ times per year.

4. Industry turn average is _____ times per year.

5. Going rate is _____ .

6. I estimate _____ units will be sold.

7. _____ (number of units) at £_____ will cover my fixed costs.

8. Top price possible is £_____. (This estimate is based on the customer's perception of value.)

Comments:

Figure 5.7 *Site evaluation*

By:_____ Date:_____

1. How will the site affect your business?

2. How does the appearance of the building affect your business?

3. Does the shop's or office's appearance complement your business's image?

4. Do you (or can you) use the location to your best advantage? How?

5. Should you move or consider moving? Why?

6. Is the neighbourhood changing? If so, how? How will it affect your business?

7. Is the site high- or low-rent?

8. Is the rent competitive for the area?

9. If your site is low-rent, how will you attract customers?

10. Is the location good from a competitive viewpoint?

11. Is the traffic sufficient for your sales objectives?

12. Will neighbouring shops help to draw customers?

13. Is parking adequate? Would paying for customer parking make sense?

14. Can you develop additional traffic? How?

15. What disadvantages does the site have? How will you overcome them?

16. Is this the best site available for your business? If no, why not?

Figure 5.8 *Checking on the competition*

By:_____   Date:_____

Competitor:_____

Location:_____

Rate 1 (poor) to 5 (excellent)   **Rating**   **Comments**

1. Appearance and design of store

2. Employees' characteristics:

    A. Telephone manners

    B. Courtesy

    C. Helpfulness

    D. Appearance

    E. Product knowledge

    F. Ability to handle complaints

    G. Ability to cross-sell

3. Availability of products

4. Convenience of location

5. Added services (delivery, etc)

6. Other (specify):

Figure 5.8 *Checking on the competition*

By:_____   Date:_____

Competitor:_____

Location:_____

Rate 1 (poor) to 5 (excellent)   **Rating**   **Comments**

1. Appearance and design of store

2. Employees' characteristics:

    A. Telephone manners

    B. Courtesy

    C. Helpfulness

    D. Appearance

    E. Product knowledge

    F. Ability to handle complaints

    G. Ability to cross-sell

3. Availability of products

4. Convenience of location

5. Added services (delivery, etc)

6. Other (specify):

Figure 5.9 *Pricing objectives*

By:_____ Date:_____

Product/Service:_____

Refer to Figures 5.3, 5.4, and 5.5 on pages 73 and 74 and to Figure 5.5 on page 77. Fill in one of these forms for each product/service.

My pricing objectives are	This objective will accomplish	My time frame for reaching this objective is
1.		
2.		
3.		
4.		
5.		

Figure 5.10 *Sales practice objectives*

By:_____   Date:_____

Product/Service:_____

My sales practice objectives are	This objective will accomplish	My time frame for reaching this objective is
1.		
2.		
3.		
4.		
5.		

Figure 5.10 *Sales practice objectives*

By:_____   Date:_____

Product/Service:_____

My sales practice objectives are	This objective will accomplish	My time frame for reaching this objective is
1.		
2.		
3.		
4.		
5.		

Figure 6.1 *Management audit*

By:_____ Date:_____

Based upon my analysis of the business, I believe that the operation is being run satisfactorily in the area of:

	Yes	No

1. **Sales and marketing**
   A. Pricing
      Are prices in line with current industry practice?
      Is your pricing policy based on your cost structure?
      Have you conducted price sensitivity studies?

   B. Market research
      Have you identified target markets?
      Do you segment your markets?
      Have you identified customer wants/needs?
      Do you know how your markets perceive your products/services?
      Has your business taken advantage of market potential?
      Has the competition been analysed?

   C. Personal selling
      Are your sales practices satisfactory?

   D. Customer service
      Is customer service a priority?
      Is there a rational balance between serving your customers' needs and
         good business practice?

   E. Advertising and public relations
      Do you select media for measurable results?
      Is your advertising consistent?
      Does your advertising budget make sense in terms of the level of
         business and its anticipated, planned growth?

   F. Sales management
      Are sales people and outside agents properly directed in their duties?
      Do you establish individual sales goals?
      Do you provide adequate sales support?
      Are your sales people trained?

	Yes	No

G. Market planning
Do you have a marketing budget? _____ _____
Do you have a market plan? _____ _____
Has your business taken advantage of market opportunities? _____ _____

2. Business operations

A. Purchasing
Are reputable, competitive vendors used? _____ _____
Do you have a purchasing programme? _____ _____

B. Stock control
Do you know what your stock turn is? _____ _____
Is slow-moving stock managed? _____ _____
Have you established rational reordering policies? _____ _____

C. Scheduling
Do goods and materials move through the business without hang-ups
  and problems? _____ _____
Do you know how long each job should take? _____ _____

D. Quality control
Are inferior incoming materials returned to vendors? _____ _____
Are reject rates minimised? _____ _____
Do you have a 'do it right the first time' policy? _____ _____

E. Business growth
Has your business grown at least above the rate of inflation? _____ _____
Have you met your asset growth, sales, and profit goals? _____ _____

F. Site location
Do you have the right business location? _____ _____

G. Insurance
Do you have an annual insurance review? _____ _____
Are the proper risks to your business (and to yourself) covered? _____ _____
Do you put your insurance package out to tender every year? _____ _____

	Yes	No

3. Financial

A. Bookkeeping and accounting
Are your books adequate?
Are records easy to come by?
Can you get information when you need it?
Do you have monthly profit and loss accounts?
Do you have annual financial statements?

B. Budgeting
Do you use a cash flow budget?
Do you use variance analysis monthly?
Are capital equipment purchases budgeted?

C. Cost control
Are cost items managed?
Are high cost items treated separately?
Is the budget used as the primary cost control tool?

D. Raising money
Have you been successful in raising capital when it was needed?

E. Credit and collection
Do you know your C&C costs?
Is your current policy successful?
Do you review C&C policies regularly?
Do you have a management policy on debtors?

F. Dealing with banks
Is your relationship with your bank open and friendly?
Do you have access to more than one source of financing?

G. Cost of money
Do you compare the cost of money (interest) with your profit ratios?
Are interest rates and loan conditions appropriate?

H. Specific tools
Do you know and use:
1. Break-even analysis?
2. Cash flow projections and analysis?
3. Monthly profit and loss accounts?

	Yes	No
4. Balance sheets?	————	————
5. Ratio analysis?	————	————
6. Industry operating ratios?	————	————
7. Tax planning?	————	————

4. Personnel
A. Hiring
Has the right mix of people been employed? ———— ————
Do you recruit from a pool of qualified applicants? ———— ————
Do you maintain a file of qualified applicants? ———— ————

B. Training
Are your employees suitably trained for their jobs? ———— ————

C. Motivating
Do your employees appear to enjoy what they are doing? ———— ————

D. Enforcing policies
Does there seem to be logic and order to what goes on in the business? ———— ————
Are reviews and evaluations performed on schedule? ———— ————

E. Communicating
Are people informed and brought in on decisions? ———— ————
Do you create opportunities for employees to set their own goals? ———— ————

5. Administrative management
A. Record keeping
Are records of past transactions and events easy to find? ———— ————
Are records retained for at least the minimum legal period? ———— ————
Is access to personnel files limited? ———— ————

B. Problem solving
Are there few unresolved problems? ———— ————

C. Decision making
Are you decisive? ———— ————
Is there a chain of command? ———— ————

	Yes	No
D. Government regulations Are you aware of local and government regulations that affect your business?		
E. Leadership Do you actually take charge of the business and its employees?		
F. Developing subordinates If you were to die or suddenly become disabled, is there a ready successor?		
G. Business law Do you have a working knowledge of applicable business law regarding contracts, agencies, sale of goods, and so on?		
Do you know how current contracts and other legal obligations affect your business?		
H. Dealing with professionals Do you have and use an accountant, solicitor, and business consultant?		
Do you use outside advisers?		

Figure 6.2 *Good management scorecard*

	Yes	No
1. We operate with a complete and up-to-date business plan which includes:		
A. One-year and three-year projections		
B. A capital budget		
2. We operate with an annual marketing plan which includes:		
A. Specific sales and profit goals, and timetables		
B. Strategies and tactics for the next three years		
C. Budgets, forecasts and benchmarks		
D. A sales plan		
Our marketing plan also includes:		
E. The demographics of our target markets		
F. A well thought out definition of the markets we serve		
G. A definition of the needs/wants our products and services fill		
H. An analysis of the growth potential of our markets		
I. A competitive analysis		
J. A definition of our 'Unique Selling Proposition'		
K. Projections for other products or services that could be developed		
L. Timetables for research and development		
3. We use monthly budgets and statements which include:		
A. Thorough and up-to-date records		
B. Cash flow budget		
C. Profit and loss account		
D. Balance sheet		
E. Variance analysis		
F. Ratio analysis		
G. Standard cost comparisons		
H. Cash reconciliation		
4. We have developed an information base that allows us to:		
A. Keep track of new developments in the industry		
B. Obtain and study key trade information		
C. Understand what 'state of the art' means in this business		
D. Provide customers with the best available information pertaining to our products and services		
E. Keep all our employees adequately informed		

	Yes	No

5. I'm certain that the business is properly capitalised since I:
   A. Base capitalisation on worst-case planning
   B. Have emergency funds (or access to them)
   C. Have discussed this with my bank

6. I understand the value of the business because I've made use of:
   A. Professional appraisers
   B. Present-value methods to evaluate terms
   C. Professional tax planning advice
   D. Accurate, timely financial information

7. We strive to improve production, quality and operations by:
   A. Keeping the plant in top condition
   B. Maintaining safe conditions
   C. Establishing high standards
   D. Standing behind our products/services
   E. Not tolerating shoddy performance
   F. Working for consistency
   G. Using our company's 'look' as a statement to our markets

8. Our personnel decisions are based on humane, carefully considered policies which include:
   A. Checklists to make sure objectives are clear
   B. Communication to make sure objectives are understood
   C. Written job descriptions
   D. Regular progress and performance evaluations
   E. Fair recruitment practices
   F. Fair wage scales

9. As for my own managerial skills, I work hard to:
   A. Develop my problem-solving abilities
   B. Stay calm always
   C. Be objective
   D. Avoid investments in my own ego
   E. Listen to my employees
   F. Plan changes in our course to minimise negative effects
   G. Make decisions promptly
   H. Get the facts behind problems always
   I. Accept my own limitations
   J. Delegate tasks that can be done more efficiently by someone else
   K. Analyse all available options

L. Develop my reading/study habits   —————   —————
M. Improve my skills   —————   —————
N. Consider and evaluate risks   —————   —————
O. Be positive with customers, employees, and associates   —————   —————

Figure 6.3   *Strengths and weaknesses*

By:_____   Date:_____

List your business's strengths and weaknesses. Use Figures 6.1 and 6.2 as guides. Give very brief descriptions and categorise each as 'internal' or 'external' by ticking the appropriate column.

Strengths	Internal	External
1. _____		
2. _____		
3. _____		
4. _____		
5. _____		

Weaknesses		
1. _____		
2. _____		
3. _____		
4. _____		
5. _____		

Figure 6.4 *Analysis of a specific strength or weakness*

Fill in one of these forms for each strength or weakness.

By:_____   Date: _____

Describe the strength or weakness. Be as factual as possible.

_____

_____

_____

What are the probable results of this strength or weakness?

_____

_____

_____

What should I do to capitalise on or correct this?

_____

_____

_____

_____

Set dates for implementation and review.

_____

_____

_____

Figure 6.4 *Analysis of a specific strength or weakness*

Fill in one of these forms for each strength or weakness.

By:_____ Date: _____

Describe the strength or weakness. Be as factual as possible.

_____

_____

_____

What are the probable results of this strength or weakness?

_____

_____

_____

What should I do to capitalise on or correct this?

_____

_____

_____

_____

Set dates for implementation and review.

_____

_____

_____

Figure 7.1 *Promotion audit*

By:_____ Date:_____

Do you: Yes   No

Know where new business is coming from?   _____   _____
Keep track of referrals and thank the sources?   _____   _____
Track advertising and direct mail responses?   _____   _____
Spend advertising budgets in proportion to your product
  mix?   _____   _____
Project a strong, consistent image in all materials, livery,
  stationery and so forth?   _____   _____
Have a professionally designed logo?   _____   _____
Sell benefits to customers in all promotional material?   _____   _____
Know what has worked, what has not worked and why?   _____   _____
Have a yearly advertising, public relations and
  promotion plan?   _____   _____
Involve your entire staff in the promotional process?   _____   _____
Advertise to your staff as well as to your markets?   _____   _____
Have strong relationships with media people and
  advertising professionals in your community?   _____   _____
Assign one person to make sure your plan is implemented?   _____   _____
Have a professionally designed 'facilities brochure' which
  explains who and what your business is?   _____   _____
Follow up promotional efforts with selling on other items
  (if appropriate)?   _____   _____
Have professional window and point-of-sale displays?   _____   _____
Analyse your probable competition in connection with the
  direct and indirect sales promotional methods you plan
  to use?   _____   _____

For any 'No' answer, you have another reason to use a professional advertising/public relations/promotion agency.

Figure 7.7 *Advertising/Promotional questions*

Ask and answer these questions:

1. Markets

   What is your market mix?

   What percentage of your business comes from:

   Individuals?

   Small businesses?

   Big businesses?

   Local trade?

   Regional trade?

   National or international trade?

   What is the market potential?

2. Products/Services

   Are they:

   Innovative?

   Specialised?

   Diversified?

   Commodity?

   Packaged?

   Tailor-made or customised?

(Answer 'how' to each 'Yes' answer.)

3. Image

   Would you describe your business as:

   Formal?

Informal?

With a community focus?

With a regional or national focus?

Aggressive?

Relaxed or laid-back?

Sophisticated?

Domestic?

Specialised?

General in outlook?

Does this description fit the way you want to be perceived as well as the way you see yourself now? Or do you want to change your company's image?

4. Business strengths

What special expertise or experience do you have?

Does your business offer:

Long establishment in the community?

Convenient location?

Outstanding service reputation?

Other benefits? (specify)

5. Competition

How do you compare with your competition's:

Market share?

Image?

6. Customer base

Do you sell:

Many products and services to a few loyal customers?

Several products to a narrowly defined industry?

Single products to a diverse client base?

Do you have a data base to tell you:

The product mix for each customer?

Where their business came from (referral, advertising, etc)?

The basic demographics of your markets?

Figure 8.1 *Problem-solving worksheet*

By:_____   Date:_____

1. What is the problem? Cite standard and variance from standard if available.

2. Possible causes:

3. Interim solution:

Figure 8.2 *Personal and business goal summary*

Personal goals include non-financial goals as well as financial goals. Limit the goals to
the most important.

1. List your personal goals.
   A.
   B.
   C.
   D.
   E.

2. List your business goals.

	For next year:	In three years:
Quantitative goals:		
A. Sales (£)		
B. Sales (unit)		
C. Profit (£)		
D. Profit (% sales)		
E. Market share		
F. Company net worth (£)		
G. Number of employees		
Qualitative goals:		
A. Market position		
B. Kind of business		
C. Target markets		
D. Business culture or style		
E. Other (specify)		

3. Potential conflicts between personal and business goals.

4. Comments

Figure 8.4 *Checklist for strategic planning*

This checklist presents a range of small business strategic options proved in hundreds of applications.

Past	Current	Future	Strategy	Probable consequences, risks
			Sample marketing strategies	
1.			Rationalise distribution. Cut back to most efficient network; look at volume, geography, type.	Increase profit margins, reduce stocks, some costs go down; may need new investment; moderate risk.
2.			Develop the market. Create demand for a brand new product.	Very high marketing costs, may increase debtors, impacts profit and loss statement, hinders cash flow; large expense budget; high risks – but high reward if successful.
3.			Penetrate the market. Increase market share: lower price, broaden product line mix, add service and sales personnel, increase advertising.	Increases marketing and sales expenses, need for working capital, and need for capital investment if capacity grows. Reduces short-term earnings; high risk.
4.			Promote new products to present market. Develop, broaden or replace products in product line, sell to present market.	Lower unit costs; increase stock, sales volume, profit and cash flow; some capital investment needed, increased development, design and manufacturing costs; moderate to high risk.

Past	Current	Future	Strategy	Probable consequences, risks
5.			Seek new markets, same products. Expand existing markets by geography (abroad) or type for existing products.	Increase sales volume and profit margins as unit costs drop and as new market grows; higher short-term selling costs; modest capital investment, increased working capital; high risk.
6.			Develop new products for new markets. Invest in developing, manufacturing and marketing products unrelated to product line for new markets.	Will increase sales volume, costs, profits (if successful); will have some problems as a new business if products unrelated to current line; will need more working capital, may need new capital investment; increase in sales and marketing costs; high risk.
7.			Rationalise market. Prune back to most profit-able segments, higher volume segments; concen-trate marketing focus.	Reduce sales volume, increase profit margins, reduce working capital needs, increase cash flow as per-centage of sales, decrease debtors; willingness to accept lower sales totals; moderate risk.
8.			Maintain products and market share. Business continues as before; same products, same markets.	Increase at industry growth rate with stable, short-term profit margins; decrease working capital and increase cash inflow over time; may reduce unit costs; investment in strategies to hold position; low risk.

Past	Current	Future	Strategy	Probable consequences, risks
			Sample management strategies	
9.			Cut costs. Reduce costs uniformly through management edicts.	Increase profit margins, achieve lowest possible returns of all efficiency strategies; needs excellent implementation to apply intelligently; moderate risks due to arbitrary nature of cutbacks – may have invidious consequences.
10.			Abandon unit. Sell or liquidate unit because it doesn't fit in with company – or because it is worth more to someone else.	Improve cash flow from sale of assets, create possible morale problem in rest of organisation; low risk.
			Sample financial strategies	
11.			Rationalise product line. Narrow profit line to most profitable items.	Reduce sales volume, improve working capital, profitability, may lead to underusing assets in short term; hard to give up old winners; low to moderate risk.
12.			Pure survival. Cut down to meet most adverse conditions by eliminating or paring down some aspects of the business.	Reduce sales volume, considerably reduce costs, improve ROI short term, improve cash flow temporarily; courage needed, moderate risk due to possible loss of market share, some danger from creditors and other trade sources.

Past	Current	Future	Strategy	Probable consequences, risks
13.			Pause in action. Slow down or establish a one-year moratorium on new capital investment; normal maintenance of business.	No effect on sales short term, may disrupt growth plans, weaken business over long term, decrease sales and earnings if pause is too lengthy; courage and large measure of steadfastness; low risk.
			Sample production strategies	
14.			Improve technology. Improve operating efficiency through techno-logical improvements in physical plant, equipment, or processes.	Decrease variable costs and increase fixed costs – an overall reduction can considerably increase profits, affects sales volume slightly; low to high capital investment; low to moderate risk depending on the extent to which the particular technology is proven.
			Sample operating strategies	
15.			Improve methods and functions. Invest in new ways of doing existing tasks by adding new 'soft' technologies; eg, new patterns of work flow, CAD/CAM, production planning and inventory control, etc, to improve effectiveness and/or efficiency.	Improve operating performance, improve functional rather than product costs; expense investment; creative thinking needed; low to moderate risk.

Figure 8.5 *Personal and business goal summary*

1. List your personal goals.
   A.
   B.
   C.
   D.
   E.

2. List your business goals.

	For next year:	In three years:

Quantitative goals:
   A. Sales (£)
   B. Sales (unit)
   C. Profit (£)
   D. Profit (% sales)
   E. Market share
   F. Company net worth (£)
   G. Number of employees

Qualitative goals:
   A. Market position
   B. Kind of business
   C. Target markets
   D. Business culture or style
   E. Other (specify):

   _____

   _____

3. Potential conflicts between personal and business goals:

4. Comments:

Figure 10.1 *Marketing action plan*

By:_____   Date:_____

Strategic objective:_____

Action steps	Target date	Person responsible	Results